SISTER, SAVE YOURSELF!

SISTER, SAVE YOURSELF!

Direct Talk about Domestic Violence

LINDA H. HOLLIES

Foreword by Marie M. Fortune

THE PILGRIM PRESS CLEVELAND

DEDICATION This book is dedicated to every victim of domestic violence who no longer has a voice. This book is dedicated to the long-term, compassionate, and effective ministry of Rev. Marie Marshall Fortune and the FaithTrust Institute of Seattle, Washington. Marie and her staff have provided the framework for ethical and pastoral perspectives to help both clergy and lay people to become vocal advocates who can offer practical responses to ugly situations. This book is dedicated to every bodacious advocate, shelter, and agency that provides the means whereby women and their children can be freed and saved. Finally, this book is dedicated to every abused individual who will decide, by the amazing grace of Almighty God, to leave a violent situation and become a survivor!

The Pilgrim Press, 700 Prospect Avenue, Cleveland, Ohio 44115, thepilgrimpress.com

Printed in the United States of America on acid-free paper
10   09   08   07   06   05   5   4   3   2   1

Library of Congress Cataloging-in-Publication Data

Hollies, Linda H.
    Sister, save yourself! : direct talk about domestic violence /
Linda H. Hollies ; foreword by Marie M. Fortune.
        p. cm.
    Includes bibliographical references and index.
    ISBN-13: 978-0-8298-1731-7 (alk. paper)
    1. Church work with abused women.   2. Family violence—Religious
aspects—Christianity.   3. Wife abuse—Religious aspects—Christianity.
4. Spiritual healing.   5. Women—Religious life.   6. Women—Conduct of
life.   I. Title.
BV4445.5.H65 2006
261.8'327—dc22

ISBN-13 : 978-0-8298-1731-7
ISBN-10 : 0-8298-1731-X

CONTENTS

*[Peter said,] "Save yourselves from
this corrupt generation."*

—Acts 2:40

*"If the cabin pressure should change, air masks
will drop from the overhead compartment.
In order to assist others, please put your oxygen
mask on first, then you can assist small children
and others around you."*

—Adapted from flight attendants'
  instruction to airline passengers

*won't you celebrate with me
won't you celebrate with me
what I have shaped into
a kind of life? i had no model
born in Babylon
both nonwhite and woman
what did i see to be except myself?
i made it up
here on this bridge between
starshine and clay,
my one hand holding tight
my other hand; come celebrate
with me that everyday
something has tried to kill me
and has failed.*

—Lucille Clifton

Foreword

"But no one ever comes to me with this problem . . ."

This is still the response of too many clergy when asked if they address domestic violence in their congregations. If we have not heard about it, it is not because it isn't there in the pews. If we have not heard about it, it is because we have not spoken about it. So the sin of domestic violence (and some would argue whether it is indeed a sin) has remained hidden from the light, passed from generation to generation.

Victims of domestic violence either have not sought the help of their church or have sought it and been sorely disappointed. Out of ignorance, some clergy have told battered women to go home to their abusive husbands, keep the family together, and pray harder. Some of these women are now deceased, murdered by their husbands or boyfriends.

Ignorance is no longer an excuse for pastors. We know or should know that domestic violence is happening to those we have been called to lead and protect. The silence is being broken by courageous survivors who share their stories and ask the church to stand with them.

Clergy are not supposed to be experts. We are the generalists who often are the critical link between the need or crisis and professional community-based services. If we *speak* about domestic violence (from the pulpit, in the newsletter, in religious education, etc.) we will *hear* about it from the individuals who are facing it every day in their homes. In this moment, we are faced with the Samaritan choice: shall we, with the priest and Levite, pass by on the other side of the road or shall we stop and attend to the injured person and provide safe shelter?

Since the early 1970s, there has been a sea change in public awareness and response to domestic violence. In law enforcement, the judiciary, health care, and other areas, much has changed to promote early identification and intervention. The church too often lags behind, more worried about maintaining the appearance of an intact family than about the health and well-being of its most vulnerable members.

As church, we are called to see and believe and to bring our enormous spiritual and material resources to bear in concert with the wider community. It takes a village to stop domestic violence. We can and must provide the moral leadership and ministry of presence so that lives and families may find healing—so that one day domestic violence will be a rare, peculiar fact of life in our villages.

Rev. Dr. Marie M. Fortune

Founder of FaithTrust Institute,
author of Keeping the Faith:
Guidance for Christian Women
Facing Abuse

OPTIONS,
ALTERNATIVES,
AND CHOICES

"Choose this day whom you will serve" (Josh. 24:15). Joshua challenges the people of Israel to make a determination about God. From the beginning, the people of God have been created with free will and the power of choice. We are intelligent human beings, created in the divine image of God and granted the ability to choose from among a variety of little gods or to select the only wise and Sovereign God. Joshua wanted folks to voice their actual choice. "Choose, today!"

God created the world as a gift to a group, as yet unformed. Different types of animals, flowers, grasses, fish, and mammals were already in place before we arrived on the world's scene. There were myriad trees, plants, and vines, all blooming and blossoming before we got here. God loves variety and there was plenty of it awaiting our formation.

Every created entity was diverse in both form and function. Every species was unique and distinct. The colors of the universe were different. The sounds were not alike. The smells and feel were not uniform. The rhymes and rhythms of the world, although in sync and in harmony, were a vast array of differences! Oceans, lakes, rivers, and creeks were flowing. Birds, flying insects, and clouds were to move freely in the air. Trees were to wave in the breezes. Animals were to walk and run. Some were given the ability to creep, crawl, and slither. Dew and, later, rain and snow had to fall. The sun had to rise. The moon had to glow. There was variety, yet there was harmony within the created order of God's universe.

It was a perfect creation. All things were created in harmony, working together to give glory to God.

Harmony. A pleasing sound. Harmony. An orchestrated movement that provides pleasure. Harmony. The arrangement of individual components working together, moving toward one goal. Harmony. Melodies being produced to inspire, to motivate, to bring together a soothing sound that stills unrest, drives discord away, calms anxiety, settles upheavals, and restores balance and order to chaos. Harmony.

The question before us is what wiped out God's harmony? Where is world harmony to be found? What does national harmony look like? Who, besides the heavily medicated, almost sedated, can claim inner harmony? When will there be harmony within our local congregations? How can we achieve harmony within our families, our homes, and our communities? How do we develop harmony within ourselves? God gifted us with a world in harmony. What happened? Where is it?

Of course, we can agree that sin, evil, the forked-tail devil, Satan, or whatever other names we have for the fallen angel of light, is responsible for the disruption of God's harmony within the created world. But on this side of the resurrection, harmony is again available through Christ Jesus! We, called by the name Christian, are now obligated to "seek peace and pursue it" (1 Pet. 3:11) and to then offer God's harmony to a chaotic and disturbed world.

We, the born again, Holy Spirit filled and led people of God, are called to be vessels of harmony. We are to be those who offer reconciliation in our places of the world. We are to bring peace as we arrive upon the scene. We are to restore harmony out of the discord we encounter with the various melodic strains that we offer by way of our words and our actions.

It's my firm belief that I am to live in harmony with creation. It's my conviction that my God-given right is to see harmony, pursue it, live in it, and for all of it to reign in my life. Life will bring some issues, some situations, and some circumstances where my harmony is violated. It is then that I have to make a new and different choice for my life. I have determined to choose harmony every day, all the time, and in all places. Whenever violence begins to rise, I have to look for and then turn toward a place of harmony. The church didn't teach me this—life did!

What is the note of harmony that I have been assigned? What tune am I to carry around and to play in the orchestra of life? As we meet and share in relationship, what note have *you* added? Each of us has a distinctive pitch that we play. Do our notes add to the confusion or do they foster harmony? There is enough disharmony in the world. Our job is to play the notes that would sound like God's beauty.

Some years ago, the United Methodist Women asked me to teach a summer study on violence. I thought that I needed to research violence in America for the class. I discovered that God was waiting for me to discover and to study the violence within myself!

We live in a violent society. Domestic, community, media, and national violence is so interconnected and pervasive that it seems normal! In the movie *The Exorcist,* a priest tells why he left the organized church. During the Nazi invasions, one day as he was praying, a Nazi shot a little girl in the head and announced, "God is not here today!" Indeed, this soldier was telling the truth! For God is not the author of violence. God created harmony. And when we are silent when we witness domestic violence, "God is not here today!"

Discord is the sound of the enemy! When faulty notes are playing, loudly or out of sync, the wrong notes are being read and heard. Although there are many diverse notes, varying syncopations, and differing scales, harmony prevails as a well-executed piece of music is played. The composer, arranger, and conductor are well attuned to any and every discordant note! Within God's musical of life, harmony can prevail. We must each be mindful of our part! And we must be willing to use the options that are before us.

Therefore, the Apostle Paul prays for us: "May the God of steadfastness and encouragement grant you to live in harmony with one another, in accordance with Christ Jesus, so that together you may with one voice glorify the God and Father of our Lord Jesus Christ" (Rom. 15:5–6). This is an appeal to unity and harmony among believers. Yet, it is not an appeal for us to stay within violent and harmful situations!

I am well aware that I have not always had an appreciation of nor did I seek out different perspectives, opinions, and outlooks from those that I had formed. Yes! I did think that I had the best idea! Yes! I did feel that my way was right! But I discovered that my way often brought discord. I thought that with my actions I could change others. But it became apparent that I could not force all the people to follow my ideas all the time. Ouch!

I discovered that I could only change myself, and this required all of my time. It took much time, prayer, and consecration. It also requires the daily presence of the Holy Spirit working in and on me to be Christ-like when I am involved with those of differing opinions. Yet I am learning that I have alternatives, choices, and options about how I state my beliefs. They ensure that I can keep the music of God flowing smoothly. This lesson enables us to see that we must find other methods as we go about the business of being God's people in community. Jesus Christ has already prayed for our oneness—our unity and our harmony in the body of Christ that is the church. Now Paul comes and prays for us again. For it is essential that we work in unity and not settle for simple uniformity.

I was born into a family where family units stood the test of time. Women in my family prided themselves on staying with their husbands "until death we do part." Divorce was a curse word. Staying together was a matter of family pride. It was a gloating point for Robinson women. So I was taught from a very early age to "get married and to stay married." The rule was: "When you make your bed hard, you just turn over more often." This was the spoken word, not the inferred word. This was written upon the schematic of my very being. Likewise, the church reinforced this as an important and essential value. Education supported this value: "Be all you can be; be a good wife." Politics supported this value: "Man and wife," as if the male owned the female as a possession. My community supported the value. It became a cultural norm.

It was madness. It was wrong. And it was not for my or any other woman's best good! It was aimed at uniformity. But uniformity only works well in the land of Perfect!

One weekend I had the opportunity to teach/preach/worship in a congregation out of state. When I arrived at the conference, the lights and heat in the building were off and remained so during my stay. The host pastor had gone out to seek alternative methods of lighting and heating the building. Fortunately, we had church as planned. During this small crisis, I asked God what the lesson was for me and that church. The wisdom I received was that all of us need to be on the constant lookout for how we can quickly and smoothly move into a different mode, an alternative mindset, and another thought pattern when it becomes evident to us that disharmony is rearing its ugly head. Too many of us have only one track that we like to run on. "I'm like this because my Mama/Daddy was like this." But Mom or Dad being hell-raisers does not fly with God! As adults, we now have alternatives, choices, and options, for we have access to the resurrection power of the Holy Spirit.

We are new creations in Christ Jesus and all the old "family" stuff is now null and void if it does not bring glory to God. Mama's bad attitude and Dad's cussing ways have got to go! Mama and Grandmama's value that said I must remain in a living hell of domestic abuse had to go! For I discovered that domestic violence was not of God. I had a right to live in harmony.

We are required to bring harmony to all of our ways and most of us need to begin practicing the various other forms that we have denied or ignored until now. What peaceable method will you practice in the coming week? Often when domestic violence is the issue, we must leave the situation in order to rediscover harmony. Our safety and that of our children is of primary importance. What strategy would you employ to bring harmony into that stressful situation? How can you do something different that will amaze your family? At your dinner table? In your house over the next week? Harmony is what God is calling for in these last and evil days.

Look around you and open your eyes to see the peacemakers in your world. What about their character and their role modeling can you steal, borrow, practice, imitate, and make yours? I have *learned* how to place my finger over my mouth, as if I am really pondering a situation. In all honesty, it's a habit I have acquired to keep my mouth shut! I've *learned* the art of self-talk. This means that even while my husband, Mista Chuck, is fussing at me about something I have done wrong, instead of flying off the handle, I tell myself, "It's alright. Let him have his piece. You know that he really does love you and would kill a brick for you!" As I do this, a smile comes to my face and my attitude settles down right away. God is depending upon me and *you* to be the bringers of harmony to our world. God desires that we live in harmony within our world. The disharmony of domestic violence is a sin!

My sister, my goal for every woman is that she is saved in Christ Jesus, sane in mind, sober in body and spirit, and safe in her environment. Harmony provides all of these elements within her boundaries. Chaos, pain, confusion, beatings, yelling, threats, and any form of battery are not of God! Yes, we do need to work on how to deal with effective conflict resolution. Yes, we do need to address the issues of stress, overload, and anger. Yes, we do need to find out where the safe and quiet places in our community are located where you can just sit down, cry, think, and calm down. When domestic violence involves physical, sexual, emotional, psychological, mental, and spiritual abuse, we need to seek a place of harmony.

I challenge you to allow the notes of peaceful harmony to dwell within you, to rule your life, and to brighten your world. God will be so pleased. So will those with whom you come in contact as you play the note of harmony assigned to you.

This book has a three-fold purpose. The first is to address some of the false theology that we have received within our local congregations. I want to have you walk with me, discern with me, and stretch with me. Let's see how together we can save our lives by unpacking some of the teachings that have kept us from searching for other options, choices, and alternatives. I want to walk with you through the creation story as we look at God bringing us back to life. I want us to rethink our communion—the sacred act that we learned represents the "death" of Jesus Christ. And I want us to reconsider the Prayer of Jesus as a place where liberty begins.

On April 6, 2005, Dr. Marie Fortune and hundreds of clergy across denominational lines joined in a national declaration to proclaim, "with one voice, as national spiritual and religious leaders, that violence against women exists in all communities, including our own, and is morally, spiritually, and universally intolerable. We acknowledge that our sacred texts, traditions, and values have been misused to perpetuate and condone abuse. . . . We draw upon our healing texts and practices . . . our religious traditions compel us to work for justice and eradication of violence against women. We call upon people of all religious and spiritual traditions to join us."

Second, this is a teaching book that will help you effectively to reach out to another sister whom you will encounter along life's journey. I want to outline some strategies, many of them from Dr. Marie Fortune's FaithTrust Institute, as well as others that I have found along my journey to inner healing. Victims and survivors of domestic violence are all around us. We just need to open our eyes and see, open our hearts to receive, and open our minds to learn how we might walk better with one another.

Within this work, I will outline what I consider to be an expanded version of the "normal and customary" definition of domestic violence. My attempt is to have us consider some psychological, spiritual, emotional, and mental acts that have violated women in the name of church and God—even in the biblical stories. This work is not a "tool" of Dr. Fortune and the Institute, although I pray that it will supplement what she so capably teaches. However, I'm making a serious case for my life experiences, my seminary training, my doctoral research, and my clergy conversations, counseling sessions, and spiritual direction activities to help us to explore multiple ways that we have been made victims of abuse within the local church.

Last, but certainly not least, this book is dedicated to *you!* I'm so thankful that you decided to take this journey with me. It's a pleasure to have you along. May the Creator of harmony, the Good Giver of options, choices, and alternatives, surround us as we travel. I guarantee you that this will be another eye-opening experience!

Remember that I am on the journey with you. Shalom, Harmony Seeker, God's best Shalom!

Acknowledgments

I give honor to God, who has given me life, liberty, and the full pursuit of my personal destiny. God called me but allowed me to be born in a very dysfunctional family. I love them all. God also called me to ministry and provided me with educational opportunities, including the ability to attend Garrett-Evangelical Theological Seminary and United Theological Seminary, along with two years of clinical pastoral education. I discovered my own dysfunction and was led to seek inner healing for my soul. I spent two additional years in clinical pastoral education at the Catherine McCauley Health Center in Ann Arbor, Michigan, with a heavy concentration at Huron Oakes, the substance abuse treatment center.

My parents were both of the Pentecostal faith and this is where I received my formative religious foundation. I was taught that God was male. I was taught that my father was the head of the family just as God is head of the church. My mother was a very dysfunctional role model, allowing her voice to be silent as my father spoke for both of them. When my father began sexually molesting me, my mother remained silent. When I finally confronted her at the age of forty, she confessed, "I didn't want to know. I needed him to love me." They both stole the essence of my innocence from me. I was their daughter, their little girl, the child who was given to their care by God.

Marian Lovelace, in Marie Fortune's book *Sexual Violence: The Sin Revisited,* provided for me the framework for their sin!

STOLEN, NOT LOST

You stole my unquestioned belief in God's Love; the preciousness of solitude in God's presence. You stole the joy of coming together to share Communion; my reverence for the deep meaning of a church family. You stole my ability to be quiet and hear God's voice and my belief in the phrase "God answers prayers." You stole my ability to find comfort in going to confession. You stole my innocence and twisted my trust in humanity. You stole my hope for a better tomorrow and instilled doubt. You stole my belief of life and wanting to live. You stole my belief in the basic goodness of people. You stole a significant part of my childhood and adolescence. You stole my desire to become a loving adult woman. You stole my voice and my actions that screamed a loud, "NO." You stole my right to claim my justifiable anger at abuse. You stole my right to easily risk council without suspicion. You stole the inner peace I experienced entering God's house. You stole many treasures and the blame and guilt is yours. Someday you will answer to God for your many thefts. Today, I leave the responsibility at your feet, where it belongs. . . . I will grieve those stolen gifts that will always be blemished. I will strive to be wiser and not cynical because of your thefts. I will go forward strengthened in faith as I know the truth—so many of my precious treasures were stolen, not lost![1]

I know a "double-teamed" type of domestic violence from a personal stance. My very first book, *Inner Healing for Broken Vessels,* is my testimony of incest by my father, a pastor in a local congregation. I honor Lynne Deming, who in 1991, as editor of the Upper Room books, told me, "We won't make you rich, but, we will make you famous." She told me the truth—I have not become rich! Yet I truly give God thanks for the influence of that first book, which has led me, step by step, book by book, to this one. For I promised God that when I saw wrong, I would raise my voice. So, this work is the result of many years of watching women being abused within the church, of hearing their pain as they came to me as pastor, as friend, and as pastoral counselor and spiritual director at WomanSpace.

My call to ordained ministry within the United Methodist Church has been both a gift and bane. I am thankful for the pastoral and administrative experiences that have been mine and I am fully aware of the abuse that has been perpetuated against me and many other women in the name of God. The church is a family whose institutional rules remain locked and rigid, "What happens in this house, stays within this house. Keep the secrets." But my call to ordained ministry is mixed with and impacted by my compulsion to save women from the wounds that I have experienced in my life. Therefore, this book is a shout out for all the domestic violence survivors in God's house who have gone on to make better lives for themselves and for their families. This book is also written for every domestic violence victim in God's house who either left in pain and desolation or who continues to bear the wounds and the scars.

Therefore, I give God thanks for this ministry of writing that The Pilgrim Press has afforded me over the past years. Lynne Mobberly Deming brought me into this family when she was publisher of The Pilgrim Press and the press published *Taking Back My Yesterdays*. To my editorial director, Kim Martin Sadler; my copy editor, Kristin Firth; current publisher, Timothy Staveteig; associate editor, Monitta Lowe; marketing department folks, Michael Lawrence and Aimee Jannsohn, and production staff, Janice Brown and Robyn Nordstrom—thank you. I give great thanks for all of their capable assistance and investment in my ministry of "writing the vision and making it plain," so that those who are running for their lives might read and understand.

In 2005, Rev. Marie Fortune, prolific author and founder of the FaithTrust Institute, received a grant from the Department of Justice to call together both clergy and lay advocates for intensive training in the area of domestic violence at her headquarters in Seattle, Washington. I had the great fortune to attend the training. My insights on the issue of domestic violence were greatly enhanced. I learned how to take my knowledge of this matter and combine it with Rev. Fortune's extensive work. I knew that this combination would enable me to make a permanent and positive impact in my world. Before I left Seattle, I made another new covenant to speak up about the issue of domestic violence within God's church.

I want to acknowledge the sisters at my "training table" in Seattle, who added so much depth to this work: Rev. Daisybelle Thomas-Quinney of Montgomery, Alabama; Rev. LaSandra Dolberry of San Diego, California; Rev. Carolyn Wilkins of Lansing, Michigan; Rev. April Christian from Dallas, Texas; Rev. Beverly Kirby from Clarksville, Tennessee; Rev. Theresa Herwynen, Sioux City, Iowa; and Rev. Claudetta Braitewaite, San Diego, California.

Finally, I must acknowledge the strong, encouraging, and enabling sistership of Rev. LaVerne Hall of Seattle, Washington, who has hosted me three times for preaching and teaching purposes. Owner of Holiday Hall Boutique and facilitator of the Northwest Clergywomen's Association, LaVerne introduced me to Rev. Neshella Mitchell. Rev. Mitchell, founder and executive director of Abundant Life Ministries in Seattle, is the epitome of a stellar sister. She worked diligently to save herself from the domestic violence waged against her by her ex-spouse, a preacher! It was a long, harsh, painful, and tedious journey, but Girlfriend, shows us—live and in living color—what success looks like when combined with the love of God. Her tenacious and determined faith to be free and her intellect of education helped other sisters to save themselves! To God be all the glory!

Of course, I acknowledge my siblings who also survived the domestic abuse of our home: Jacqueline Donna Brodie-Davis, Alberiene Adams-Morris, James Donald Adams Jr., Regina Camelia Pleasant, Eddie Eugene Adams Sr., David Joel Adams Sr., and Robert Tyrone Adams.

I acknowledge my loving spouse, Mista Chuck Hollies, and my children, Gregory Raymond Everett, Grelon Renard Everett, who died in 2004, and Grian Eunyke Hollies-Anthony, who have each survived my episodes of craziness! And I acknowledge the investment into my life by my grandparents: Dock and Eunice Wade and Lucinda Weston; my loving aunts, Lessie Bell King and Ethel Kellom; along with my very best and most long-term friend in all of the world, Barbara Jean Baker-Vinson-VanBuren; my faithful friends Darlene Sims Lee, Rev. Janet Hopson, Rev. Constance Wilkerson, and the Rev. Dr. Dennis Robinson, who all await my arrival on the other side!

I'M THROUGH CRYING!

I'm through crying,
and feeling the intense pain in the pit of my stomach,
and reaching for distant arms that aren't there,
and looking for the wind to answer unanswerable questions,
and talking to brick walls,
and screaming for the help that was inside of me all along,
and trying to please an unpleasable being,
and trying to measure up to standards beneath me,
and settling for less than I deserve.

I'm through crying
and shaking from fear of being left,
for being left, abandoned, betrayed, lied to, forsaken,
violated, abused,
and trying to understand someone who doesn't understand
themselves,
and fearing being strong and assertive and determined and
all the things that make me who I am, a queen,
and compromising my royalty to an unfaithful subject for his
love that never existed in the first place,
and being tired,
and being tried,
and forsaking who I am, what I am and Whose I am,
and searching for a heart that has no heart at all.

I'm through crying,
and blaming myself,
and letting others blame me for something I didn't do,
and accepting the blame to carry the peace,
and wanting the blame so he can feel better about himself,
and compromising the blame to compromise myself to compromise

my heart, my soul, my body to someone who neither deserved
the thought, the energy, nor the sleepless nights, nor the
anxiety shivers, nor the anorexia, nor the depression, nor
wails of "What did I do???"
and prolonging the inevitable ending of two people, on
different levels,
on different planes, on different planets, on different
capacities, on different, different, different.

I'm through crying,
for nothing,
who is nothing,
what is nothing,
nothing from nothing leaving nothing,
for the nothing he gave,
for the nothing promises he spoke,
for the nothing support he administered,
for the "I love you's" he knew nothing about,
for the nothing love he couldn't give because he only read
about in books and saw it on television—a worldly love,
so common, so overused,
so outdated, so quickly distorted, so instantly said, so much
full of nothing.

I'm through crying,
and forgetting who I am,
and forsaking who I am,
and letting him tell me what he claimed was wrong with me,
and letting him insult me, belittle me, tear me down,
and accepting his mental, spiritual, and emotional abuse.

Lord, God, Creator, forgive me for placing an insignificant
man in front of you,
and tolerating someone who was intolerable,
and being a good woman to someone who doesn't deserve me,
and overexerting my love to the limits and destructive
expectations of his cruelty,

and giving all of myself to someone who couldn't appreciate a morsel, let alone deserve a limb of my kindness, my care, my compassion, my passion, my goodness, my patience, my longsuffering, my unconditional love, my favor.

I'm through crying![2]

—*Phenessa Gray*

1

SISTER, ASSESS YOUR CONGREGATION

They were women then
My mama's generation
Husky of voice—stout of step
Hands
How they battered down
Doors
And ironed
Starched white
Shirts
How they led
Armies
Headragged Generals
Across mined fields
Booby-trapped
Kitchens
To discover books
Desks
A place for us
How they knew what we
Must know
Without knowing a page
Of it
Themselves[1]

When the words, "the black church" are voiced, there are three powerful words that immediately come to mind: women, music, and preaching. In some denominations, black women are not able to be ordained and/or are not able to officially lead congregations because of the continued patriarchy that is both preached and practiced as God's will. Nevertheless, the fact still remains—without women there would be no church! For "in the beginning," God ordained that it would be Mother Eve who would carry "the church" within her womb and bring it forth as the eliminator of the conniving, deceitful devil!

What too many fail to remember is that the world was formed in Africa! The Garden of Eden and all of its inhabitants were dark-skinned people who multiplied and moved into all other parts of the known world. Eve was a woman of color. Generations later when her "child" arose from the dead, it was another woman of color, Mary Magdalene, who met him as the gardner and was given the mandate to go and tell the disciples that resurrection had occurred!

God called Abram and Sarai to leave their home, in the area we now know as Iraq, and take off with little family and few belongings to "found" the church that we know today. Abram and Sarai were called to establish a new family that was to become more numerous than the sands and the stars. When God seemed to be a bit slow in blessing them with the family that they desired, Sarai suggested that her slave, Hagar, a woman of color, become mother to Abram's firstborn son. Ishmael, known as the heir to Abram's estate, was born. This is one of the primary cases of domestic violence recorded within Holy Scripture. When Sarai finally became pregnant with her child, Isaac, she had Abram drive Hagar away. This is another case of domestic violence! For Hagar was sent away, forced out, and rejected from the "family" that she had known and in which she had been a central character.

God has promised, "My house shall be called a house of prayer!" God's house is always to be a sanctuary. God's house is to be a safe place and a sacred space for all, even the foreign born. Both Abram and Sarai broke God's covenant of hospitality and oppressed Hagar. This was sin.

An angel met Hagar in the desert and sent her back home when she tried to flee from the abuse. But at Isaac's birth, Abraham, whose name had been changed by God to "father of many nations," gave Hagar a loaf of bread and a jug of wine and sent her away for good.

While in the desert, lying under a bush, crying, with a son she thought might die, Hagar was visited by God, who came to provide her with water and to give her the very same message of inheritance through multiple children that Abram had received! "Do not be afraid; God has heard the voice of the boy where he is. Come, lift up the boy and hold him fast with your hand, for I will make a great nation of him." (Gen. 21:17b–18) Hagar is the "mother" of the Muslim religion, just as Sarah became the "mother" of the Jewish nation. God has never allowed or permitted women to suffer domestic violence without providing a way of intervention and often escape. God has never had a problem with using women to advance the realm of Jesus Christ. This pattern has proven true down through the ages.

The very first conference for women was called by a young nameless woman, only known as Jephthah's daughter and recorded in the eleventh chapter of the book of Judges. Annually, the Order of the Eastern Star uplifts her example as the epitome of faithfulness to God. This young woman's father sacrificed the "first thing" that came out of his home in a deal with God for winning a victory for his tribe. She was, however, the only child who greeted him, and she only asked for three months away with her sister-friends before she willingly submitted to being sacrificed. This is another horrible case of domestic violence in Holy Scriptures!

This young woman of color gave great inspiration to Nannie Helen Burrough, who in 1906 led the movement for what we now know as National Women's Days in the National Baptist Church. Anglo churches do not celebrate these annual church days. But, to uplift the work, self-worth, and ministry of women, Mrs. Burrough wrote:

> A million women praying? A million women singing? A million women desiring? A million women laboring for the coming of the kingdom in the heart of all, would be a power that would move God . . . it would mean spiritual dynamite that would blast Satan's greatest stronghold and drive sin to its native health. . . . We are in desperate need

of women learning to become public speakers, and dedicated to a definite cause for which to speak. . . . Women's Day was intended to raise the women themselves—training them for public speaking and informed leadership through authentic, prepared challenging speeches. . . . The day offers a glorious opportunity for women to learn to speak for themselves!"[2]

When the apostle Paul arrived in Macedonia in northern Greece, he sought places where he could preach the good news. It is recorded in Acts 16:13–15 that "On the sabbath day we went outside the gate by the river, where we supposed there was a place of prayer; and we sat down and spoke to the women who had gathered there. A certain woman named Lydia, a worshiper of God, was listening to us; she was from the city of Thyatira and a dealer in purple cloth. The Lord opened her heart to listen eagerly to what was said by Paul. When she and her household were baptized, she urged us saying, 'If you have judged me to be faithful to the Lord, come and stay at my home.' And she prevailed upon us."

This woman of color was an astute business person, an entrepreneur who assisted the spreading of the church among the Gentiles. Paul was not ashamed to list her attributes and contributions, and he also named many other notable women in his list of greetings and thanksgivings in Romans chapter 16. The extended missionary work, the in-depth compassion that led to the work of deaconesses and nuns all are due to the ministry of women in the early church. Yet the church has continually used the writings of Paul to oppress, restrict, and assist in violence against women in the name of God!

The new church in Philippi had several notable women of color in leadership. It is recorded by Paul in Philippians 4:2: "I urge Euodia and I urge Syntyche to be of the same mind in the Lord. Yes, and I ask you also, my loyal companion, help these women, for they have struggled beside me in the work of the Gospel . . . whose names are in the book of life." Relationship issues among women continue to plague congregations today due to the subordinate roles and fragmented leadership allowed women in the black church. It is too often the misinterpretation of sacred scripture that prevents black churches from allowing women to be as liberated today as they were with Paul. Nothing that Paul wrote spoke about men abusing their wives and children!

As a matter of fact, Paul instructs spouses to love their wives as Christ loves the church. This is in direct opposition to the domestic violence that is perpetuated in some congregations.

Gilkes concludes her work with these striking words:

> The picture for women in ordained ministry within the historically African-American denominations is not good. Ironically, there are two contradictions at work among Black professionals and white churches. Other Black professional men, particularly in male dominated professions such as medicine and law, have no problem affirming the leadership of Black women; electing them to the presidencies of the National Medical Association and the National Bar Association as well as to the presidencies of other professional, clinical, and academic associations. . . . The churches with the greatest mass appeal in Black communities, facing the greatest crisis, have thrown up the greatest barriers to women's empowerment in their national bodies and local congregations. Yet, churches in Black communities are more female than male."[3]

Ordination in some historically black denominations is very restricted. Yet it has been women who have taught the masses in Sunday schools, vacation Bible schools, and mission departments. Further, women have chaired major fund-raising programs to support institutions such as historical black colleges. Women have led choirs, sang songs, and composed songs that tell the theology of the black church. In other words, women "run" the house of God! If women from any denomination were to collectively take a Sunday off, there would be few congregations with congregants to worship.

The matter of domestic violence dictates that we pause to consider this silent subject within God's church. Far too many

Christian women are being abused physically, sexually, emotionally, and in some cases spiritually, in the name of God! Far too often, the pastoral counseling of the past has focused on family reconciliation—regretfully, at the expense of the well-being of a woman and/or her children. Thankfully, with education, training, and the growing number of statistics that report violence against women, many counselors are no longer giving bad advice to women—especially if there has been physical abuse.

The book *God Don't Like Ugly* by homiletics professor Teresa L. Fry Brown provides much insight into the leadership of women of color. It successfully uses the medium of song. She reveals the unspoken secret that in subtle and quiet ways women of color have always led within the black church. The songs are used to celebrate community, detail ritual practices of worship, share the history and experience of a people, and tell who God is and how they think about God. Throughout the period of traditional and contemporary gospel music, black women—Sallie Martin, Clara Ward, Doris Akers, Lucie Campbell, Roberta Martin, Mahalia Jackson, Mattie Moss Clark, Aretha Franklin, Tramaine Hawkins, Margaret Douroux, Sandra Crouch, and Sweet Honey and the Rock—have been prolific "preachers" in song! Gospel music is biblically based and its lyrics are not tied to one particular time period, subject, age, gender, denomination, or racial or ethnic group.

For example, in 1970 Margaret Douroux wrote "Give Me a Clean Heart." The song is about the need to change one's behavior in order to be of service to God. Understanding the difficulty of living in a world that negates ones' existence or expresses hatred rather than love, Douroux writes, "Lord, fix my heart so that I may be used by thee. . . . Please give me a clean heart so that I may follow thee." The song is based upon Psalm 51:10: "Create in me a clean heart, O God, and put a new and right spirit within me." This song relates to God's power to transform our minds and emotions. Furthermore, it talks about being amenable to God and not to the praises of humanity.

"Music provides a critical opportunity to teach or to share community values and beliefs. The majority of choirs are made up of women and youth who 'rehearse and remember' the theology, spirituality, and beliefs of their denominations primarily under the direction of women musicians and teachers. . . . The images and characteristics of God in gospel music are transmitted Sunday after Sunday from choir stands and in congregational singing."[4] Yet, with all of our songs, there are few that dare to address the pains, hurts, and wounds of women.

"Why cannot we do something to distinguish ourselves, and contribute some of our hard earnings that would reflect honor upon our memories, and cause our children to arise and call us blessed? Shall it any longer be said of our daughters of Africa, they have no ambition, they have no force? . . . How long shall the fair daughters of Africa be compelled to bury their minds and talents beneath a load of iron pots and kettles?" These questions were asked by Maria Stewart in Boston in 1832! "Unnamed millions of Black women have urged their sisters and daughters to make the world know that they have lived rather than merely become statistics in actuarial charts. They have suggested that women live a Christ-like life; become president, or own their own business."[5]

Now the time has come for women of Christ to stand up, to testify to their experiences, and to call out the unnamed millions of women who are being subjected to domestic violence in its multiple forms. It is time for Christian women to make a conscious decision that "they may have life, and have it abundantly" (John 10:10)!

Women have started entire denominations, built churches, and kept the doors open until a male preacher/pastor could come along and take the lead. In her book *Sisters in the Wilderness: The Challenge of Womanist God-Talk,* Dr. Delores Williams provides us with a full account of the many women who have walked the desert journey of Hagar and birthed churches in their wilderness experiences.[6] Ida Wells Barnett led the antilynching movement. Mary McLeod Bethune, a graduate of Moody Bible Institute, was a known street preacher who founded Bethune College, which today is called Bethune Cookman College. She served the nation under the presidency of Theodore Roosevelt. Mary Church Terrill was noted for founding women's "clubs," which helped to uplift the aspirations of women. Harriet Tubman delivered enslaved Africans to freedom; Sojourner Truth and Maria Stewart were great antislavery "preachers." Rosa Parks became known as the mother of the civil rights movement. All of these women are noted for their inspired leadership among women of color. Their leadership greatly affected the world. Each woman used her own unique style to make a permanent and positive impact upon our lives. They were pastors without titles, without ordination, and without permission!

We know that woman can pastor churches. We know that women can lead institutions. We know that women can become dynamic entrepreneurs. We know that women have divine destiny and live lives of purpose. Yet women must throw off the oppressed mentality that is forced upon them by the institutions of culture, religion, marriage, education, judicial systems, and misinterpreted scriptures. The Bible is "good news." This book is not about violence for church women in every aspect of life. This book speaks about the good news of freedom. Therefore, finding ways to talk about domestic violence within God's house is mandatory for all of us!

A must-read book about the leadership roles of women in the black church is *Open Wide the Freedom Gates!* It is the personal memoir/autobiography of one of the matriarchs of our nation, Dr. Dorothy I. Height. Dr. Height was called to ordained ministry as a young woman. In 1924, young, gifted, and black, she tried to enroll in New York Seminary but was denied access. Graduating from New York University after being denied entrance to Barnard College, which was directly across the street from New York Seminary, she went to work at the YWCA and learned all that they could teach her about administration. Then the time came when she felt led to accept the call of Dr. Mary McLeod Bethune and take leadership of the National Council of Negro Women. She was "pastor" of this august group for forty-one years, majoring in the text of civil and women's rights. With a background in the principles of the YWCA, she has worked unceasingly to be in the forefront as an advocate for the safety and liberty of every woman.

At the installation service of the Reverend Dr. Suzan (Sujay) Johnson-Cook, as the first female "pastor" of the ten-thousand-plus member Hampton Minister's Conference, Dr. Height gave her testimony and passed Sujay her mantle of leadership, authority, and female advocacy. It was a high moment where no male had to preside! Again without "official" permission—and without apology!— Dr. Height, Mrs. Coretta Scott King, and presidential candidate and former Senator Carol Mosely Braun all gathered to signify that the black church continues to be led by women. There are new voices on the scene. We will not be silent. And the issue of domestic violence, even within the house of God, is one of our agenda items.

The black church has a great legacy of strong women who have persevered despite the sexism that continues to prevail. Black women have never faltered in their determination to serve God, uplift their nation, and lift others as they climb. It is now time for those of us who are called to be "trumpets in Zion." We must lift our voices and give the clarion call that domestic violence within God's house is a sin. No longer will we be silent! No longer will we stand by and act in concert with the violators. May it be so now and forever, for it is the divine will of the Ancient of Days!

REFLECTIONS

- What are your responses to any new facts about domestic violence?

- How are women being treated in the local church that you attend?

- How were women treated in the local church of your childhood?

- In churches today, do you see, experience, view, or have witness of any "better" treatment toward women?

2

SISTER, GOD CALLED US VERY GOOD

But a woman who fears the Lord is to be praised. Give her a share in the fruits of her hands, and let her works praise her in the city gates.

—Proverbs 31:30–31

She was nobly fashioned by the Divine Designer. She was created, not born. She sprang from the soil, but she had originated from above. She was fashioned out of dust; but she was inspired by the Triune's celestial breath. She was a friend to creatures; but she was the offspring of the Sovereign God. This beautiful new creature was placed in the delights of Eden. It was a beautiful and fertile garden with light and pleasant occupation; but she had responsible duties. She was gifted with immortality, intelligence, instincts, and speech. She was God's crowning creation, who was invested with world dominion and trivial restrictions. She was not Jehovah-Elohim, who is supreme and ultimate. Nor was she simply an animal, created too low, without the power to think or to choose. She was not, in the first creation story in Genesis 1, created after Adam. Nor was she created to be subject to or inferior to Adam. According to the second creation story of Genesis 2, she was the last of God's handiwork. Presumably, therefore, she is the best thing that God ever created! She had to be the crown of all visible creation. Woman is her name!

God had created the very best home for her reception. God had made provision for her total maintenance. God gave her beauty to be appreciated, a body to be admired and intellect to be respected. She was a gift and a present to the world. She was "the" added attraction. She was the cream of the crop. She was given claim to the full allegiance of her man. She was promised love, affection, wholesome sex, and protection from the beginning. Time, leisure, and approval were to be her allotted gifts in life. She was to be held dear and near to the heart of her husband. Woman was her name! Nowhere is there room for permission from God for domestic violence of any sort against women!

Woman. The "isha" of Hebrew, taken from the word, "ish," for man. Woman. The real glory of Adam, the man. Woman. The delight of heaven. For it is after her that the church of the Living God is named. Woman, the virginal and the pure, was made for clinging to and mating with one man. He was to fulfill her every sexual, emotional, and physical need. Woman.

The mystery that gives blood like Jesus Christ is woman. For without the shedding of innocent blood, there is no remission of sin. Yet, during her fertile days, when a woman stops her monthly bleeding, it is to create new life. And when she has lived long enough to cease the monthly flow, that blood is stored within herself to be used as energy for re-inventing and re-creating herself. Woman was not designed for violence but for life abundant.

Woman, the full wisdom of God. Woman, the fatal folly of fools. Woman, the joyful and the joyless astonishment of the human male world. For all across the world, women are continually restrained, oppressed, and misunderstood. Woman, the indissoluble character in a marriage whose very image, alone, should condemn the practice of polygamy and adultery. Woman, the softer and gentler character of nature. Woman, who will cry in both joy and in pain. Woman, she will give and dares to take back. Woman, she is wife, mother, sister, friend, confidant, and foe, all wrapped into one flesh. Woman, she is bone, flesh, and intellect combined. In the second creation story she was created last so that she might be put first, and she was called woman!

For ages, the world has asked the question found in Proverbs 31: "Who can find a woman of virtue?" And for ages men have overlooked what is right under their noses. For ages, men, irrespective of color, have taken women for granted. They have overlooked their wives at home while seeking other relationships. Women have taken care of men, put up with their mess, and had their babies. Women of virtue have been among us all the time, loving hard and sometimes hardly being loved!

If it were not for women, there would be no historic black colleges and universities. If not for women, there would be no growing and thriving churches. If not for women, there would never have been a savings and loan institution owned by people of color nor any NAACP to benefit humankind. If not for women, the AME Church in Los Angeles would not have been founded while Juneteenth was yet trying to find enslaved black folks in the West.

If not for women, there would be no hair care products for women of color, no hair combs, hair brushes, or body creams for blacks. If not for women, there would be no new and improved South! For while white men were dreaming, planning, and working outside their homes in industry, manufacturing, and economics, it was black women who were raising their children, cleaning their homes, and making sure that a decent meal was on their tables.

As we look around us and remember the women who are responsible for our existence, "Who can find a woman of virtue?" is an insane question. When we dare to recall the struggles, the sacrifices, and the self-giving, self-denying, and self-killing ways in which women whom we call Mama, Ma Dear, Big Mama, and Grand, struggled to give us life, we have the answer to this ancient question. Clearly, we can tell from the question that a woman's perspective, our answers, nor our lives were taken into consideration when the Bible was compiled.

The Bible is a record of stories that were told according to the needs, personalities, and position of Jewish men. In every culture, the status of men is uplifted above that of women. So we must approach the reading of scriptures with this knowledge. If you would dare to look at the first book of the Bible, you will find another story outlined that does not look like the one in chapter 2.

This book of beginnings is not history—as we know it—for there were no human beings to record the creation. We know that the beginning is not simply some scientific myth according to Darwin's theory of evolution, where humans emerged from apes. Therefore, we are left to concur that the Genesis account of creation is a tale of revelation, handed down by oral tradition and recorded by Moses, the friend of God.

Every culture enjoys a good story. There are numerous creation stories told by every culture. While we were in school, we had to learn about the Greek gods and goddesses and all of the Roman myths. We may remember Pandora's Box, which is another version of the creation story. However, the Genesis text, and particularly chapters 1 and 2, are both inspired creation stories. Please go and find your Bible. Open it and turn to the first chapter of Genesis. It begins, "In the beginning, God."

Elohim, the strong and mighty one, is known as "Bereshith," the same who emerged from eternity for the commencement of time. And, by word of mouth, this Bara, interpreted as the Highest Being to be reverenced from "ex nihilo," out of nothing, produced everything we now call the heavens and the earth. The heavens is where God, the Trinity, and the ever-praising angelic host dwelt on earth. A terrestrial globe with both atmospheric elements and firmament were both created by the One Who Holds Eternity!

There was chaos, desolation, and no population in the formless, lifeless, shapeless, objectless, and tenantless form of matter until Elohim, the Creator, spoke. In the midst of an opaque shroud, thick gloom, no order, and no life form, the Spirit of God moved upon the face of the waters. It was the Ruach of Elohim, the life-giving Spirit with wind and breath, that began the initial movement that slowly advanced and began a great transformation. Out from eternity God stepped and God spoke. It was the beginning of time.

The evolution of the cosmos was accomplished by a series of divine formative works that extended over a six-day period. Ten different times we hear the powerful words: "And God said . . ." God spoke, and every time the divine essence breathed out a word, it was followed by instantaneous movement. For the Living Word is creative all by itself.

God spoke and we see the beginning of light separating the opaque—in which God had dwelled. God spoke and we get air and water. God spoke and we see dry land and plant life. God spoke and there were both the greater and lesser celestial lights, followed by fowl and fish. God spoke and the animal kingdom was created. Everything possessed the potency of life that is the ability to reproduce itself. And God said, "It is good."

Everything was now ready for the magnum opus, which was to close the creative labor of the Sovereign and be the foreshadowing of the marriage between Jesus and his bride, the church. There was a concillium among the Trinity as the construction of this new creature was being considered.

"Let us make *humankind*, in our image, according to our likeness," states Genesis 1:26, "and let *them* have dominion over the fish of the sea, and over the birds of the air, and over the cattle, and over all the wild animals of the earth, and over every creeping thing that creeps upon the earth." Verse 27 says, "God created humankind in his image, in the image of God he created *them;* male and female he created them."

In verse twenty-eight, "God blessed *them,* and God said to *them,* 'Be fruitful and multiply, and fill the earth and subdue it; and have dominion over the fish of the sea and over the birds of the air and over every living thing that moves upon the earth.'" Verse 29 states, "and every tree with seed in its fruit; you shall have them for food." Verse 31 concludes with the full cosmos being given a glorious benediction, " God saw everything that he had made and indeed, it was very good."

We find that woman, the symbol of God's church, along with her mate, was given body image, reason, beauty, intellect, erect stature, a soul, and a moral nature. Together, they both were created as spiritual beings with moral integrity and holiness. They had free agency and were given dominion over creatures. They were both given rule and supremacy. Three times it is said that God created *them,* male and female, on the sixth day. And the Creator pronounced that both of *them* were exceedingly good, beautiful, and excellent. They were without fault, blemish, or sin. Here, in chapter 1, it is both the male and the female who are created together and given equality by God. There is nothing here to signify God's granting of domestic violence as a right of either partner. Nor does scripture suggest female inferiority or domination. Go back and read it again!

In the creation of the human couple, we find God's resolution is a great work. In the creation story, we see God's forethought. All else was executed with Word instantaneously. But, there was divine handiwork involved in the making of Adam and Eve. They needed personal care and attention. There was divine delight in fashioning them in the divine image.

This couple has kinship to the Godhead. This couple was made in a heavenly image and likeness. And this couple was given the *imago dei* or a resemblance to the divine image. Both the man and the woman were given personality, purity, power, intellect, and wisdom to become representatives of God. They were visible embodiments of the Supreme as they walked among the lower creation.

When the creation was complete, God instituted the sabbath day for rest. Both creation stories agree on this. There are, however, several differences that we must recognize. In the first creation story of Genesis 1, we see that God produces vegetation at will (Gen. 1:11). In the second chapter vegetation depends upon rain, mists, and agricultural labor (Gen. 2:5–6). In Genesis 1:7, the earth emerges from the waters and is saturated with moisture. In the second story, earth appears dry, sterile, and sandy. Finally, in the first story man and woman are created together, while in Genesis 2:7 the man is created first with the woman being later extracted from his body in verse 22. Most often, male preachers will mix these two stories together for the benefit of male domination, making woman the rib/helpmate. Reread both stories!

In the first story, Adam bears the image of God. In the second story, his earth-formed body is animated by the breath of life and he is placed in Eden to cultivate and to guard it. In the first story the birds and the beasts are created before the humans. In the second story the man is created before the beasts to name them. You must choose what story best fits your theology. We are forced to deal with the differences. As well, we need to investigate and to wrestle with Woman Wisdom's creation story in Proverbs 8:22–31.

What we have is an internal unity between all three creation stories. God is the creator, and we are the result of God's creation. We also have divine bestowment of life formed from mere dust. This life is placed in a garden environment where all that humans need waits for their arrival. Therefore, we can deduce that what we find is the startling fact that the church is a divinely prepared female creature. She is exceptional in her glory and prophetic as a woman—a woman called Wisdom, in both stimulating our hope and stimulating our faith, while being assigned our work to be fruitful and multiply.

There is a four-parted river in the Garden of Eden that corresponds to the four gospels of Jesus Christ. It is the gospel, the good news, of Jesus that spreads hope. It is the gospel, the good news, of Jesus that brings healing. It is the gospel, the good news, of Jesus that sheds light and gives life. And it is the gospel, the good news, of Jesus that enables us to rejoice in the love of community! In the Garden of Eden there is a tree whose fruit is good for the healing of the nations. In the garden were placed a man and a woman who were to remain sinless and perfect. In the garden were placed a man and a woman with a marriage covenant. "Therefore, a man leaves his father and his mother and clings to his wife, and they become one flesh" (Gen. 2:24).

Ephesians 5:22 picks up this marriage covenant as it begins, "Wives, be subject to your husbands as you are to the Lord." Verses 25–27 adjure, "Husbands, love your wives, just as Christ loved the church and gave himself up for her, in order to make her holy by cleansing her with the washing of water by the word, so as to present the church to himself in splendor, without a spot or wrinkle or anything of the kind—yes, so that she may be holy and without blemish." Finally, we arrive at the conclusion of the matter in verses 31–32: "For this reason a man will leave his father and mother and be joined to his wife, and the two will become one flesh. This is a great mystery, and I am applying it to Christ and the church."

It is this Ephesians passage that has been preached, taught, and quoted to too many women, causing them to return to violent partners. It is this Ephesians passage that has been a primary counseling tool used in previous eras of pastoral care and counseling. It is this Ephesians passage that has sent women back home to "try harder," to not anger their mates so an eruption of violence would not occur. Women were counseled to learn how to be more submissive by "submitting!" Fortunately, however, within this same Ephesians passage is the true liberty from domestic violence that any woman needs: "Husbands love your wife as Christ loved the church and gave himself up for it . . ."! Love does not hurt! Love heals! Why has this particular message been so silent within our churches?

The creation of Adam and Eve is the story of Christ and his bride. The creation of Adam and Eve is the symbolic message that we have for the act of marriage being a holy covenant—a life giving act between a man and a female. The creation of Adam and Eve, Jesus being the second Adam of the Spirit, and the church being called woman are permanent and visible reminders of just how much God loved, valued, and made significant the role of every woman and every marriage.

As we look at that woman who is often uplifted in Proverbs 31, we can began to better understand this portrait of a woman who is virtuous (translated in Hebrew as one of strong force), industrious (one who is diligent in her work ethic); organized (one who is able to attend to details), outreaching (one who is community minded), managing (one who is able to maintain and to save), overseeing, and including all who have needs within her grasp. This is not a passage to make us work ourselves to death. This is a passage that says this woman who is called the church had it together. The conclusion of the passage said that her spouse, her mate and partner in marriage, gave her great respect and praise. She was not beat down for not doing enough. She was praised for all that she brought to the table!

This woman, called the church, is surrounded with gifted, talented, wise people who seek to fulfill the mission and the ministry of the Bridegroom. This woman, called the church, is expected to be about the business of being excellent, of being praised by the city, of being admired by her spouse, her people, her community, and her offspring. This woman, called the church, is being watched over by her spouse because she is both loved and respected. She is appreciated. She is well applauded for her industry, her creativity, and her vision. She is a godly woman who knows the power of the Holy Spirit and uses her gifts to accomplish far more than we, as single women, can ever think or imagine! For her name is woman and she is the church of Jesus Christ! Her name is woman and she is the bride of the coming Bridegroom. Jesus gave his life for his bride. There is no record of Jesus beating on or dominating the disciples, although they vexed him severely! This is the type of love that we are to see, experience, and expect in marriage relationships and within the church of Jesus Christ, our Bridegroom!

The church, the bride of Christ, is a woman who has so many of our natural and human female tendencies. So, if we would be candid and look at our local congregation as a woman, we can better understand that in some cases, this might be the primary concern that is holding us back as well as stifling our local congregations!

One of the most destructive habits that women have is they worry too much. We spend too much time obsessing over stuff that never happens. We hold secret within us the ugly stuff that we pass off as "love."

While a woman's greatest joy tends to come from giving, in reality we give away all of our stuff for free. And we feel guilty when we cannot give away more!

As women, our greatest loss is living in a second-hand and inferior mode. We must learn how to live up to our God-given self-worth, self-determination, and self-respect. I honestly and sincerely believe the creation story of Genesis 1, where God gave every woman both power and dominion, along with every man!

The most satisfying work of the average woman is that of helping others. We, however, will help but will not ask for help when we need it. When domestic violence enters our homes, we need to seek help! There are networks, communities, and agencies committed to working with us. We cannot be both independent and interdependent. God has called God's church to community and interdependence. There are no superstars in the God's church. All of us are "stars" and every star that is not brightly shining has an issue that the rest of the community needs to work on for healing, restoration, and restitution.

Surely the ugliest personality trait that any woman can ever exhibit is that of selfishness—trying to keep all of what she has received for herself. The average woman has a tendency to not share either her burden or her power. There is, however, a time when saving one's self becomes essential! There comes a time when self-preservation is required for our lives for the sake of our innocent children. This is not being "selfish." This is being wise and using the wisdom that God has provided. Wisdom speaks to our inner power. We must remember that Jesus shared his power.

The most endangered women are those who, on the outside, are dedicated leaders while in secret they allow themselves to be maimed or killed. We know how to do so many things, and we do them so well. But we don't know how to train others to take our place for the responsibilities to be carried on when we are gone. We also do not speak truth about domestic violence. We must begin to speak the truth about this evil so that we can save others, including our children, who are watching, learning, and imitating us.

We need to recognize and cultivate the reality that our greatest natural resource is our youth. They need our attention, our teaching, and our instruction today! They think that they know it all, but we know that they do not know everything. We need to be about the business of paying attention to them and drawing them into active ministry. We must also teach them the reality and seriousness of domestic violence.

We need to teach them that domestic violence is a sin! We need to give each other a "shot in the arm" in the form of words of encouragement. If what we have to say to each other is not about building each other up, we need to learn how to keep it to ourselves. The gifts of encouragement and consolation should be spoken by each of us in the Christian church.

The greatest demon that women need to overcome is fear. For we talk with a double-edged tongue when we declare, "I can do all things through Christ," and yet fail to take action that will save our lives and the lives of our children.

The greatest gift that any woman should have is hope. The deadliest weapon to every woman is her violent domestic partner, be it spouse or child. The most worthless emotion that any woman can have is self-pity. This will get you killed quickly!

The world's most incredible computer is a woman's brain. Learn how to think issues through and do not rely on "passed-down knowledge" alone. Learn to trust your inner voice! Pray daily for "the mind of Christ."

The most power-filled words of any woman are, "I can" and "I will"! The greatest assets given to woman are her faith in Christ, her hope in God, and her belief in herself! The most beautiful attire a woman can wear is her own authentic smile—a smile that is shown on the outside and inside when she knows that she and her children are safe!

The most prized possession of a woman is her integrity. She stands on her word. The most powerful channel of communication that each woman can use is prayer. Often the very best prayer is a scream of "HELP" as she runs away from violence and into a safe environment to start all over again!

The most contagious spirit that a woman can utilize is her enthusiasm to live, and to live abundantly! Jesus said, "I have come that they might have life and have it more abundantly" (John 10:10).

The most important thing in a woman's life is her relationship with Jesus Christ, who makes her know that resurrection and rising is her constant theme of praise. And the most powerful force in any woman's life is love. Violence is not to be tolerated from anyone, anywhere, at anytime, for anything because God is love!

The church of the Living God was created by divine design. She is both a gift and a present to a dying world. Jesus gave his life and died for her. The Holy Spirit lives inside of her. Whosoever will can enter into her sacred space and receive life. Woman will have nothing to do with violence or death! For she is good and very good, and her name is woman! Thanks be unto God!

REFLECTIONS

◆ Had you ever previously seen/been taught the difference between Genesis 1 and 2?

◆ What is your opinion about women being in pastoral leadership in the church?

◆ What is your divine destiny from God? How is it being lived out in your local church?

◆ What is your knowledge of domestic violence around you? Within your local congregation?

◆ How do you feel that God looks at violence toward us, God's beloved creatures?

◆ What did this chapter teach you or present to you that you did not know or had not thought about before?

◆ After this, what will you do differently?

3

SISTER,
GOD'S LOVE IS
A TREMENDOUS
MYSTERY!

*The human contribution is the essential
ingredient. It is only in the giving of oneself
to others that we truly live!*

—Ethel Percy Andrus, social activist

In June 1990, the *Boston Globe* reported the story of a very unusual banquet. It seems that a professional woman and a wealthy man, who intended to be married, went to plan their wedding reception at the Boston Hyatt Regency Hotel. Having both expensive taste and the money to afford it, their reception bill came to more than $13,000. After leaving a check for half that amount as down payment, the couple went to get wedding announcements.

The day that the announcements were to be mailed, the potential groom got cold feet. He said to his fiancée, "I'm just not sure. This is a big commitment. Let's think about this a while longer." It was an angry woman who returned to the hotel to cancel the banquet. But the bride neglected to remember the hotel's refund policy. She was entitled to only 10 percent of the down payment.

It seemed crazy, but the more the jilted bride thought about it, the more she remembered her not too distant past, the more she recalled that once upon a time she had been hungry, addicted, homeless, and not employable. The more she recalled her own life, the more she felt like going ahead with her party. It would not be a wedding reception, but with all of the money that had been paid, it could be an awesome party.

In honor of the missing groom, the young woman changed the meat to boneless breast of chicken! But she kept everything else the way it had been planned. Then she sent invitations to all of the rescue missions and homeless shelters in the city. So on a warm June night, the Hyatt Regency Hotel in downtown Boston hosted a dinner party unlike any held there before.

On that summer night because she had remembered her own past, people who were used to peeling half-gnawed pizza off cardboard boxes and drinking and eating out of garbage cans instead ate chicken cordon bleu. It was a party where Hyatt waiters in tuxedos served hot hors d'oeuvres to senior citizens who were propped up by crutches and aluminum walkers. Bag ladies, drunks, prostitutes, vagrants, and homeless drug addicts took the night off from the hard life of the streets. Instead of having to fend for themselves, along with the woman's family and friends that night they all ate well, sipped champagne, had chocolate wedding cake, and danced to big-band melodies late into the night.

The night became an event to remember. It was a reminder to the woman of how far a loving God had brought her. It was a reminder to the street people that due to amazing, undeserved, unmerited grace, for a few hours they could glimpse the memories of their "better" life. At the big downtown Hyatt hotel, it became a reminder to the wait staff and to the administrative staff that Love always includes others. Love always draws the circle wider. For Love takes all sorts of different people and makes them family.

That night in June 1990 there was a strange and complex community who shared communion together. All of the elements of what we now call the Lord's Supper were present that night. The bread and the drink were the staples of life. The bread and the drink were a symbol of life abundant. And the bread and the drink became a holy sacrament that pointed toward life eternal.

Jesus always took the simple things of life to tell profound truths. The holy meal of communion takes an assortment of strange people and makes them community, family, and support to one another. Theologians have elected to call this sacred meal and the lavish love of God, a *mysterium tremendium*. It's a five-dollar term for what we know is the tremendous mystery of our faith. God's amazing love for a sinful world is a tremendous mystery. Why God so loved the world that Jesus was sent to die for our sin will never be fully understood by the human mind. So it has always been and always will be a mysterium tremendium within the house of God.

On the night before the feast of the Passover, Jesus decided to share a special meal with his friends on this significant occasion. He made special arrangements so they could eat the very same meal that the Jews had eaten the night they were delivered from generations of slavery in Egypt. So the very first role of the communion is to point us toward our deliverance from the bondage of sin.

God gave Moses specific instructions so that all Jews would be prepared to leave slavery at a moment's notice. Exodus 12 gives us all the details of the Passover and declares "Your lamb shall be without blemish, a year-old male; you may take it from the sheep or from the goats . . . then the whole assembled congregation of Israel shall slaughter it at twilight. They shall take some of the blood and put it on the two doorposts and the lintel of the houses in which they eat it" (Exod. 12 5, 6b–7). They were to eat the meal at home. They were not to go to the local synagogue, but they were to gather as families, with the strangers and foreigners among them, around tables.

Verse 8 outlines that the lamb was to be roasted with bitter herbs. This was a foreshadowing of the Lamb of God, who was coming to take away the sin of the world. The bitter herbs indicated that the life of Jesus and his followers would be filled with suffering. There would not be time for bread to rise with yeast; therefore, the meal required that the bread be unleavened. Likewise, the house had to be searched diligently by the women to ensure that no yeast was to be found anywhere.

God gave Moses instructions in verse 47 that no one was to eat the meal alone. If there were any circumcised single people, foreigners, or strangers in their midst, all of them would eat together as family. For salvation is in community! Finally, they had to eat with the cloak tucked into their belt, their sandals on their feet; and a staff in their hand with the meal eaten in haste. Nothing was to be leftover until morning.

The Passover meal was God's way of preparing God's people to leave years of oppression, injustice, and cruelty. God did not want the domestic violence used by Egyptians against the Jews to continue any longer. The Lamb of God is a symbol of peace. Communion is an act of leaving violence and moving into a promised land that is better! Often the family that you "eat" with is not the one that you were born into or married into. Yet there is a supportive community for each of us.

Can you begin to imagine the faith of these slaves? Can you begin to see the tremendous mystery that had to be involved with all of these rituals, all of these new rules, and all of the preparations while they were yet in bondage as slaves? They were getting ready for a new day. They were acting out of a future hope. They were preparing for new life as a free people. Their discipline to follow specific instructions was because of their tremendous faith in a Covenant God. The promise of freedom, the prospect of liberation, and the hope of deliverance kept these folks in great anticipation. It was a tremendous mystery—but following God is always a journey in mystery. For God is Ultimate Mystery who declares to us, "My thoughts are not your thoughts nor are your ways my ways" (Isa. 55:8).

When the God of Mystery came through Egypt, striking dead all of the firstborn of every home and the livestock in the land, Jewish dwellings with blood on the doors were "passed over." These homes were left alone—untouched because of the salvation of the blood covenant that God had made with Abraham and Sarah. There is wonder-working power in the blood of the Lamb of God. The "how" and the "why" is all part of the *mysterium tremendium* of the God who longed for these people to live in peace and harmony without violence being used against them.

It was this sacred and holy celebration of memory and tremendous mystery that prompted Jesus to sup with the twelve disciples. At the table Jesus sat among friends, also with an enemy, with doubters and betrayers. Jesus, the Lamb of God, sat at the head of the dining table, knowing that he, an innocent lamb, was to be betrayed and slaughtered. Yet he said to his adopted family—a group of complex, mixed-up, confused, and disbelieving disciples whom he loved so well—"This is my body. It is given for each one of you! This is the cup of the new covenant, in my blood, poured out for each one of you!" He said this in the present tense as he sat, alive and whole among them. Saying these words about flesh and blood to law-keeping Jews was certainly a tremendous mystery to them!

Jesus always used simple things to illustrate greater truths. Jesus knew that the disciples needed to eat. Eating is a requirement for maintaining a healthy body and mind. Jesus did not select things that were not common to each one in that room but decided to use bread, made from fields of wheat, as a reference to his whole body that was to be broken and given for our "at-one-ment" with God. Giving his body in place of our body as a substitute made Jesus the bridge over which we now come into relationship with God. "This is my body, broken for you." Our bodies should never be broken!

As a nation, we are a people who love to eat. We eat at any and every important occasion in our lives. For some, following a kindergarten, high school, or college graduation, we have an open house where friends and neighbors are invited to come and to eat. When we get married there is a reception where we gather to eat and to drink. When we have a baby dedication, we gather to eat. And, surely, after a funeral we look forward to the standard repast of delicious food! As a nation, we are a people who love to eat. Food and drink are staples in our lives. So we understand when Jesus called his friends together and said, "Let's eat."

After the supper, Jesus took the cup and said, "This cup is the new covenant in my blood, poured out for you. Drink this and remember me." As the people in the Wilderness of Sin were rebelling, Moses had broken the first covenant given to him by God—the covenant that had been written on tablets of stone. Jesus refers to what the disciples know as the Ten Commandments or the Law. He holds the juice made from grapes and declares that the shedding of his blood will bring about a new covenant. The shedding of his blood marks a new relationship. His shed blood allows every human who accepts Jesus as their Savior to have a new relationship with God. Giving his blood means that our blood should never be shed. God was preparing all of us for life without additional violence! Thank God for the blood of Jesus!

The blood of the Lamb of God has miraculous powers. The blood of the Lamb of God has saving power. The blood of the Lamb of God has keeping power. The blood of the Lamb of God has healing power. The blood of Jesus is efficacious, meaning that it covers, eradicates, and wipes out our sin. The blood of the Lamb of God is a tremendous mystery! It was that wonder-working blood that ran down Calvary's cross, the blood that met with the life-giving water, flowing from his wounded side. The church of God was birthed at that cross!

When the blood and the water met at the base of the cross, our sin of rebellion, our sin of disobedience, and our sin of separating ourselves from God in the Garden of Eden were thrown into the Sea of Forgetfulness. God will never remember our sin when the blood covers them and we live in holy relationship. Jesus told that little group, "This is my blood. It's poured out for you. Do this in remembrance of me."

The loaf of bread and that cup of wine—simple household staples—became the symbol of Jesus and are used by Christians to remember his death on the cross. The meal was a required staple for life. And that meal became a symbol of eternal life. For Jesus said for them to eat the meal and to "remember" him.

To remember is to recall, to call back again to memory. The Latin word *memor* means to be mindful of a thing, an event, or a person. So Jesus instructed them that as they ate the daily staple of life, the meal would cause them to recall him and his being the Passover Lamb for our deliverance from sin. Domestic violence is a sin! Jesus died that we might be delivered!

During that Passover feast, communion became an institution of the Church. During that Passover feast, although the disciples did not understand the logic, while they could not comprehend the reason why, the meaning for, the importance and significance of the words spoken and why Jesus prepared and served a meal for them, the pattern was clearly established for the way that we, the church, come together in this present day at the communion table.

At the table, Jesus is present to remind us that he rose from the dominion of sin, shame, and separation. Jesus lives! And while we are to remember his death and his suffering, we are also to work to make the church a place of salvation and deliverance for whosoever will come. For the holy meal is a staple. The holy meal is a symbol. The holy meal is a sacred sacrament of life eternal.

Before the disciples could go out and celebrate this new institution of the church, a fight broke out about who would be the greatest. The issue of power and control rose up in the midst of a family meal. Jesus was trying to tell them, show them, explain to them that he loved them and the world enough to die for them. But they got stuck on who was going to get the highest political office when he took over the Roman government. The soon-to-be church of Jesus was stuck on stupid! The church of Jesus was totally clueless. The church of Jesus had eaten the holy meal, but they didn't get the message. Power and control are not keys to the realm of God.

Domestic violence is always about power and control! It is not about God. It is not of God. And God is not in domestic violence. In Luke 22:29–30, Jesus says to the clueless group, "The world wants to run you, to oppress you, and to lord over you as rulers. But look at what I have done for you. I have loved you and I have prepared a place for you. I have given you my broken body. I have served you my poured-out blood. And now, with your crazy, confused, mixed-up selves, I want to confer upon you the authority of God's realm. I want you to become coheirs, corulers, cojudges of the world to come. I want you to be with me. And if you want to be with me, watch me and learn how to serve! The greatest among you will be the one who serves!" This is surely a *mysterium tremendium!*

To become great by serving is a different philosophical take from that of the world. To become great by serving is a quite different from battering, abusing, and controlling someone in the name of love! When we can learn how to serve one another in love, like Jesus served with agape love, then and only then will we become great people in the sight of God. To serve in love is not to argue, not to condemn, not to control, and it is not to prevent others from living the abundant life. Rather, serving in love means that we are to promote others and allow them the fullest range of freedom so they might become their very best selves.

Where are the loving, serving people in the church of God? Where are the ones who know how to "take low," step back, step aside, and allow others first place? Where are those loving and serving people who will allow others to go ahead of them in the line? Where are those loving, serving people who really do ask, "What would Jesus do?" and then just go and do likewise? Jesus came to love us, to serve us, and to give his life in exchange for each one of us. Where are the loving servers who practice what they preach in the church?

Whenever and wherever we eat the prepared Holy Meal of the Passover Lamb, we accept all of the benefits of new, resurrected life in Jesus Christ! Whenever and wherever we eat this Holy Meal we are to remember the generous love of a Lavish Creator. We are to recall that liberating, freeing ministry of generations ago, when enslaved people walked across dry land to be rid of violence and injustice. We also recall the horrible, awful death of Jesus. Likewise, we must recall that victorious Easter morning's triumph over sin, death, and hell as a crying woman, Mary Magdalene, met who she thought was a gardener in the dim light of the early morning.

This meeting where a dead body had been laid retracts the curse put on women in the Garden of Eden! (Go back and read that sentence again!) That curse laid in another garden, where Eve had been placed under the domination of Adam due to sin, was overturned, reversed, and changed! For when Mary Magdalene, the second Eve, met the resurrected Jesus, the second Adam, she was given the assignment to go and to tell the scared, hidden disciples that resurrection had occurred! *Jesus Christ reversed her curse and sent her off rejoicing!* This is the story that we need to remember, whenever and wherever we take communion.

There is great controversy in the church world about what actually happens when we eat the sacred meal. There are three primary views among theologians: 1) Some believe that the blood and the wine actually become Christ's body and blood. This is called transubstantiation. 2) Others believe that Christ is spiritually present to us, by faith, in and through the elements. And, finally, 3) all agree that the bread and the wine are lasting memorials of Christ's sacrifice at Calvary. All theories point to freedom, salvation, and life eternal.

Regardless of where we stand, the reality is that we are called to know that the Holy Meal of the church is offered to us in the mighty and matchless name of Jesus Christ! The communion elements go into our very "is-ness" and becomes the power that we need to make it through every situation. It is a *mysterium tremendium* how food, drink, or tablets know how to get to where they need to in order to do the most good for us. But as we drink and take medications, we can tell when they have done their work by the results. We know that there is a difference!

Following my graduation from seminary, I served as both a chaplain and chaplain supervisor at Catherine McAuley Hospital in Ann Arbor, Michigan. All chaplains had to do what is known as "on-calls," or be available in the evening for patients and staff. One night I got a call from a doctor about a male patient who was crying inconsolably. He was scheduled for open-heart surgery the next morning. His physician was worried about his mental health especially since all of his medical forecasts looked great. They could not understand his tears. So I was called to talk with the man and to listen.

I discovered that thirty-plus years prior, his son had been extremely ill and had to undergo extensive brain surgery. This loving father had gone to the chapel to make a deal with God. He had, in essence, asked God to spare his son's life and to take his. This crying man felt that during his upcoming surgery, God was coming to collect the prize. After his son got well, he had stopped going to church and was now a "lapsed" Catholic, with no priest to call. That night, I asked him if he loved God. I asked him if he accepted Jesus

Christ as his personal Savior. I asked him if he wanted to repent of his sin. And I told him to remember that God did not take seriously our little human deals because God is the Sovereign! Then I went into the kitchen and got an orange pop and a package of soda crackers and we had communion at his bedside. For Jesus was present to claim him, calm him down, and take him through that surgery.

Orange pop and soda crackers, you might ask? It could have been Coca-Cola and graham crackers! I often do communion with big red grapes and animal crackers. It is in remembering and praying that Jesus Christ is present and we are delivered. Jesus says in Matthew 18:20, "For where two or three are gathered in my name, I am there among them." So in hospitals, in shelters, in homes all across the world, Jesus is ready to meet us and to sup with us.

On one Sunday, a deacon saw me take and drink an open cup of consecrated juice after a woman had dropped her wafer on the floor. (We use the little quickie cups with the wafer on top of the juice.) When the deacons served communion to me, I took it again. The deacon standing closest to me asked, "Did you take communion twice?" My answer was "yes." There have been some times that I have taken communion up to four times on a Sunday! I took one for my ill son; two for my unsaved children; and one for me! I believe that I need Jesus working in me as well as Jesus working on my behalf. I know that I need the substance of the body and the blood working through my veins, through my vessels, and through all the systems of my flesh. I need the love that the Holy Meal represents working in me at all times. For this says to me, "Linda, I want you to remember me. When you are struggling with temptation, remember how I was tempted in all points like you but did not sin. When you have been hurt, abused, rejected, and forsaken, remember me. Eat this meal and remember me."

Jesus says through the Holy Meal that though the road ahead of us is unclear and though our footing is often not sure and though we don't always know the way that we should take, and sometimes we will feel as if we are alone, "Remember me. I promised never to leave you and to never forsake you! I am the Way. I am the Truth. And, I am the Life. Remember me."

To anyone of us who does not know Jesus Christ in the pardon of our sin, the Holy Meal is a call to new life. For the weight of our sin, which will become a heavy burden that is too hard for us to bear, was already nailed on Calvary's cross. All we need to do is to confess, repent, and own Jesus Christ as Savior of our lives. The meal says that Jesus has already remembered us!

Before we give consent and power to the authority of sin—within the church, within our homes, within society, and within our world—before we profane ourselves even deeper with the evils of the world, and before we devalue ourselves further in all the foolishness that destroy us, in body, spirit, and soul, we can come to the table of life. We can come to this table to eat the meal and allow Jesus to be present to us, in us, and all around us. For Jesus works on the inside, making a difference on the outside!

The Holy Meal calls us to be both a loving and a serving community. This meal calls us to unity but not to uniformity. For our spiritual gifts make us uniquely different. This meal says that all of us who receive it by faith are family. For the life-giving blood of Jesus makes us one. It makes no difference if we are crazy, mixed up, messed up, or completely insane! Jesus loves us so much that he died for each one of us and none of us are to die for another! This meal says that we are each special. We are each chosen for salvation. We are each worthwhile individuals. None has the right to abuse another!

The Holy Meal is a staple of life. The Holy Meal is a symbol of eternal life. And the Holy Meal is a sacrament for every one of us who have dead loved ones on the other side. Jesus says through the Holy Meal that death does not have the final word. The grave is not the end. "For I died and I got up just for you! Resurrection is the church's theme song of praise. One glad morning, when this life is over, those who live and believe in me shall never die. We will all eat together in eternity."

Communion is greater than any one sacred table. Communion is far more than the symbol within pretty cups and plates. Communion happens whenever we get together, in the name of Jesus, and break bread and drink together with prayer. Communion can happen whenever two or three of us get together, touching and agreeing in the name of Jesus.

Why not make the decision that you will intentionally call a supportive sister to sup together as you pray about the various needs between you? You can have communion at Wendy's, Burger King, or the local shelter with a sister and her family. All we have to do is to pray, eat, and drink as we remember the salvation and the deliverance that we have in the name of Jesus and in our meal.

It is my joy to announce that because of the Passover Lamb's broken body and shed blood, we don't have to accept domestic violence any more! Jesus freely shed his blood for all of us and his blood will never, ever lose its saving power. It's a *mysterium tremendium,* but it is also our good news!

REFLECTIONS

* What are your earliest memories of gathering with your church family for communion?

* What are your reflections about the Passover meal being God's way of delivering the Israelites from "domestic violence?"

* In your faith tradition, what is taught about taking communion?

* When have you ever had a "sacred communion meal" with a friend?

* In what ways can communion be helpful to women who are being battered?

* What did you learn in this chapter that is new to your way of thinking?

4

SISTER,
LET'S TALK ABOUT
THE "SECRET"

We are broken and will not be mended until
we remember that we are unbreakable!
Women get it. And, because we get it, we are
the mothers of peace—from the inside out."

—Louise Diamond

My brother David is a very interesting and complex man. Although I am the oldest, there are times that I turn to him for counsel because he is a trained counselor. He is one with whom I will consult about family matters because he is very sensitive, intuitive, and devoted to the family. In our adult years, he and my family have lived together for months at a time when he made the move from Florida to the Midwest. It has been in these times that I have learned a new side of my little brother.

My husband, Mista Chuck, is the master "fix-it fellow." There is nothing that Mista Chuck does not have some bit of information about, a resource reference for, or a suggestion regarding. In our living together, when David would need Chuck's help or when he ran into a situation that he could not readily master, he would not come to me—big sister that I am. He would seek out Mista Chuck and ask him, "What's the secret?"

These days, Chuck and I laughingly use this phrase when something puzzles either one of us. For "What's the secret?" implies that there is some hidden knowledge, some undisclosed clues, and some insider information that is being withheld. David's searching, seeking, and inquisitive probe for additional wisdom is exactly what the disciples did when they asked Jesus about his personal habit and method of prayer. "Jesus," they asked, "Tell us, what is the secret to the way that you pray?

The disciples and the seventy who had been sent out by Jesus were all Jews. They were familiar with the Orthodox Jewish habit of praying three times a day. They were raised on the ritual of praying. They had to memorize the prayers. They could recite the prayers, debate the prayers, and even teach the prayers to others. But there was something different, there was something powerful, something effective about the habit and the methods that Jesus used. The disciples and the seventy wanted to know, "What's the secret?"

Inquiring minds wanted to know how Jesus was able to heal the sick, cure the afflicted, and give them the authority to cast out demons. These people wanted to know just how it was that the teaching Jesus provided changed their lives and brought peace to troubling situations, and how he knew with specific details things that had not even occurred and what was on their mind. It was real clear that their habits of praying were not providing them with the power and the effect that Jesus had. So it made good sense that they would ask the Teacher of teachers to teach them how to pray as he did.

There is only one word that can conquer God. There is only one word that can unite separated souls at God's mercy seat. There is only one word that can offer us peace and safety, provide songs in the night, and lift our loads of guilt and shame. There is only one word that can provide us with strength sufficient to our daily task, lift us up when we have fallen, and make us coworkers with the Almighty God. There is only one word that can heal our loneliness, comfort our sorrows, and offer forgiveness and reconciliation for every prodigal son and daughter. That word is prayer. For James says, "The prayer of the righteous is powerful and effective" (James 5:16). When there is domestic violence around us, we need the power of effective prayer!

My dear sister, there is a secret to effective, life-changing prayer. So Jesus gave a model to those who were going to take his message to the world. Jesus provides for each one of us who are called to minister to each other a formula for effectiveness. We all need to remember and to recall that we are not alone on the journey. We all need to be reminded and to have it affirmed that there are others who are praying for us, even as we pray for them. And the prayer that we know as the Lord's Prayer or the Prayer of Our Savior is more power-packed than we realize.

Jesus had the answer to their question about effective prayer and it was based on a personal relationship, a quality relationship, and a powerful relationship with the One who invites us to pray in the first place. God is Sovereign. God is everywhere, at the same time. God is there, God is present, even weeping with us in those horrible times and experiences of our lives. It is God who has saved us time after time. It is God who is at work in us, giving us strength, faith, and the willingness to live the abundant life.

Jesus would slip away to pray. Jesus would duck the crowds to get away from people to pray. Jesus would spend the night, off alone, in prayer. The disciples saw the results of his prayer life. Many people experienced the healing effects of his relationship with God. Demons had to flee when Jesus lifted his voice in prayer, for there was all of the power of heaven behind his words. And whenever we call the name Jesus, something happens! Something happens in the visible world and something is happening in the spiritual world that we cannot see.

The Jewish community knew about the ritual of prayer. Jewish people knew the words of prayers that they had been taught. Jewish rabbis could teach the formula for prayer. But these prayers had no power. Now, after being sent off by Jesus to be involved in ministry, after hearing Jesus tell them that they were given power and authority to cast out demons, to lay hands on the sick, and to speak peace to a troubled and disturbed world, the disciples realized that there was a deeper secret to be revealed. They realized that there was more for them to learn; so they asked the Teacher of teachers to teach them how to really pray.

The first prayer meeting had been held in the Garden of Eden. A beautiful world had been created for Adam and Eve. They had a lovely world, plenty of trees, fruit, nuts, berries, and wild animals for company. They had been given latitude, flexibility, and dominion over the whole world. There was only one stipulation and that was to not eat the fruit from one tree that was planted in the middle of the garden. Well, we all know that they proceeded, just like us, to do exactly what they had been told not to do. When their eyes became open and they found that they were naked, they made fig leaf aprons and hid behind bushes to hide from God who came to visit with them every evening.

The running and hiding of Adam and Eve was the very first prayer meeting held in the newly created world. For the two humans realized that they had messed up royally! They came to full comprehension that they had broken the cardinal rule, thereby ruining, violating, and severing their personal relationship with the Almighty God. So, body bent and knee bowed, the couple, without words, began to plead for mercy. And God came to provide an answer to their nonverbal petition.

The running and hiding of Adam and Eve also set the stage for the very first act of domestic violence in the newly created world. The male creature, Adam, decided to point a finger of blame at his wife, Eve, and to blame her as the reason why he accepted the forbidden fruit. Adam took no responsibility for his own decision or action. His response to God was an act of violence toward his mate for life.

What we have to understand is that God yearns to be in relationship with us, and God longs to answer our prayers more than we are willing to pray. It is this same God who has declared, "If my people who are called by my name humble themselves, pray, seek my face, and turn from their wicked ways, then I will hear from heaven, and will forgive their sin and heal their land" (2 Chron. 7:14). What's the secret? It is keeping the way clear so that our relationship with God remains intact.

Jesus gave the disciples, and those of us who are now charged with being his representatives in the days and years and centuries to come, a formula that is guaranteed to get God's attention.

Realize that God is greater than just you and me; God is greater than a male or a female. Realize and acknowledge God as the God of all by saying, "*Our Creator. Our Protector. Our Sovereign. Lavishly Generous God,* you, who made and loves the entire world." Call upon our God by the name, the title, and the reference, even as God, my Friend, who lives far away, in heaven and whose name is holy, and yet, who is as close as the mention of that sacred name! God's name was so holy that the Jews would not mention it! They began to refer to God as Jehovah, Yahweh. There are a million and one names that we can find to refer to God. The Holy Scriptures chose to use the noun, Father. However, for many domestic violence victims, a father image is not necessarily positive, and the word does not easily fit our mouths! And since God is neither male nor female, but Spirit, we can select our own reference to the One who created us and longs for our presence in prayer!

Show reverence to God. Esteem the name of God. Do not dare to take God's name in vain. Remember that God came down from heaven and in the midst of chaos and emptiness created the world with the words, "Let there be!" This awesome God deserves and demands reverence, respect, and our worship. This Sovereign God longs for us to come close, in prayer.

Omnipotent, Omniscient, and Omnipresent One, let your will be done in me! I am merely one of the earth's creatures. Yet I am one made in your image from dust. Since you thought enough of me to create me, to form me in my mother's womb, and to send Jesus to die in my place for the sin of our original parents, help me to do what pleases you. Let your will be done in this piece of earth as it is being done in heaven where angels, archangels, seraphim, and winged cherubim stand day and night, crying, "Holy, holy, holy, the Lord God the almighty. The whole earth is filled with your glory" (Isa. 6:2). So, surely, I desire that your perfect and divine will be done in me.

Give me this day the Bread of Heaven that you sent to feed me until I want no more. Give me this day, the broken body of the Host at the heavenly banquet table, who sacrificed his life that one day I can be united with God and Christ. Give me this day enough daily bread, enough strength, and enough sustenance, and by your amazing grace I will make it through. Give me this day the Bread that will allow me to be filled with wisdom, with self-confidence, and with enough self-respect that I can live a life that is pleasing to you.

Bread of Heaven, Bread of Heaven, feed me until I want no more. For I am weak, and you are mighty. So hold me by your powerful hand and don't allow temptation to be too strong for me. My spirit is willing to follow your way, God, but my flesh is weak. Feed me until I can say, "No" to violence. Feed me until I can say, "Yes" to abundant life. Feed me so that I will not allow anyone to ever put me down. Feed me until there is a rod in my back that makes me stand straight and tall! Bread of Heaven, feed me!

God, lead me not into temptation, but deliver me from evil. Deliver me from the evil within me. Deliver me from the evil that seeks to destroy me. Deliver me from the evil and let me not be tempted to take human revenge into my own hands. Deliver me from the evil and lead me to the safe and the secure pastures that you alone can provide. God, you know all about me. God you designed me in your divine image. God you breathed into me the breath of life, so I want to be in relationship with you as well as be in healthy and wholesome relationship with my brothers and my sisters on earth.

Forgive me my sin as I forgive those who sin against me. God, I don't want to block my blessings and I don't want to "forgive" too soon or only with my lips. God, I know that healthy relationships are essential with you. God, I know that you demand that I love you with all my heart, with all my soul, with all of my mind, and with all my strength. Then, you said that I have to love my neighbor as I love myself. God, you are asking too much. God, you know how "they" have treated me. God you have it on record just what "they" have done to me. God, only you know just how much I have lost sleep, cried in the midnight hours, and hurt when I recalled their ugly and devastating words. And you want me to forgive them? There is no way! God, you are asking too much!

Did Jesus really say, "*Forgive our sins as we forgive those who sin against us?*" That is exactly what it says. And that is exactly what it means.

The entire system of salvation is established upon the word "forgive." Jesus came through forty-two generations so that he might become the Lamb of God who took away the sins of the world. Jesus did this so that all of humanity might be forgiven by God for our rebellion against God's holy directions. Without forgiveness, each one of us would be duly bound to spend eternity in hell. But with the sacrifice of Jesus at Calvary we were forgiven. Our debt was eradicated. Our slate was wiped clean. Our relationship with God was reestablished, and now we can approach God in prayer through the name, the blood, and the power of Jesus Christ. It is all about us being forgiven!

Yet, one of the biggest problems in the church is the sin of unforgiveness. Jesus is giving directions to those who are going into the world. They are being sent as sheep among wolves. They are being charged to go into the world and to deal with people who would hurt them, who would lie on them, who would stab them in their back and even kill them. Jesus knew that they were being sent to encounter a real painful existence. There was going to be deceit, betrayal, disappointment, and even the horrible pain of being sold out by a so-called friend. So Jesus said, "Forgive those who are going to sin against you, because I have to die so that you might be forgiven by God."

Forgive our sins as we forgive those who sin against us! If we refuse to forgive, we hinder our own soul. Matthew 6:14–15 states it this way: "For if you forgive others their trespasses, your heavenly [God] will also forgive you; but if you do not forgive others, neither will your [God] forgive your trespasses." It's pretty cut and dried. When we refuse to let go of the things that others have done to us, as painful or as hurtful as they may be, what we do is block all God's blessings from coming our way! Unforgiveness stands between our soul and our God! This type of forgiveness can only happen when we have moved out of the domestic violence into a safe place where we can feel and experience God's peace.

Too often we refuse to forgive because we want revenge. Too often we will not forgive because we believe that forgiveness is tied to reunion and reinstatement of the former relationship. Too often we refuse to forgive because we believe that if we forgive that we are chicken, we are punks, or we are weak. But none of these are worthwhile reasons to stay out of relationship with God. The best thing to do—the most sensible thing to do—is to lift that person from your "Get 'em list" and put them into the hand of God. God has already said, "Vengeance is mine and I will take care of them." *Human forgiveness is not possible alone.* We can not just automatically let go of the anger, the pain, and the hurt that goes along with domestic violence. But when we have moved away from the situation, we can ask the Savior to help us, to comfort, to heal, and to keep us. For Jesus is willing to help us let go of our human need for revenge and to forgive the sin against us. Jesus will carry us through. Sisters, we are each sent into the world to be representatives of Jesus. The primary work of Jesus was to win forgiveness for us; and the primary task for us is to keep our relationship with God open by continually working to forgive others as they sin against us. The secret is to always keep our anger and our hurt and our unforgiveness before God in prayer.

There is no greater day than today. Today you can let that old, ugly, acting-out anger go. There is no better time than now to determine that with God's grace, "I am going to put this unforgiveness into God's capable hand." There is no better place than exactly where you are to release that rancid garbage and to allow the Great God of Heaven to enter and fill that empty space. It simply means a wave of your hand. It only requires a nod of the head or a pat of the foot to say, "God, I need you in this matter and I am willing to give it to you now."

Take a few minutes now to put this unforgiveness to rest and to allow the Son Light of God's love to flow in your life. *For to God belongs this realm and eternity, all the power and all the glory!*

In his book *My Utmost for His Highest,* Oswald Chambers says, "Never choose to be a worker for God, but once God's call is placed upon you, woe be to you if you turn aside to either the right or the left. We are not here to work for God because we have chosen to do so, but because God has laid hold of us. What we are to teach others by our lives is also determined by God."[1]

The Lord's Prayer helps us to keep our soul steadfastly related to God. Remember that we are not called simply to convey our testimony but we are to proclaim the good news of Jesus Christ by our lives. The call of God comes with an agonizing grip of God's hand-print upon us. Our life is in the grip of God for this very purpose, to represent Jesus Christ. Jesus Christ did not allow others to abuse him! Jesus willingly gave his life for our salvation, but he lived a life of justice, integrity, and love. The life of Jesus is one where good care, time apart, family, friends, and community were all important to his life. Jesus never allowed others to isolate him for their purposes. He lived an open life and calls for our lives to be open examples also.

Chambers continues, "We cannot ever water down the Word of God, but we must practice it in its undiluted sternness. We must have an unflinching faithfulness to the Word of God."[2] And when we come to personally deal with the souls of others, especially our abusers, we are to remember that we are not some special being created in heaven. The Lord's Prayer reminds us that we too are just sinners saved by grace. When we allow others to abuse us, to mistreat us, and to speak without respect to us, we are sinners. For God created us for love! Love never hurts!

Keeping the Lord's Prayer ever before us holds the secret to a personal relationship with God that will keep us grounded in excellent personal relationships with others. We will treat them with dignity and respect. And we will only receive dignity and respect in return. The Lord's Prayer keeps both partners in responsible relationship.

I close by charging each of you to remember the words of Paul, "Beloved, I do not consider that I have made it on my own; but this one thing I do: forgetting what lies behind and straining forward to what lies ahead, I press on toward the goal for the prize of the heavenly call of God in Christ Jesus" (Phil. 3:13–14).

REFLECTIONS

- When did you learn the Lord's Prayer (the Prayer of Our Savior)?
- Who taught it to you?
- Has this prayer been prayed or sung in unison in your local congregation?

◆ Has the Lord's Prayer been a part of your daily devotions?

◆ What new information about prayer will you put into practice today?

◆ An ancient holy man of the church once said that when we pray we should use as few words as possible! What do you understand prayer to be for you?

◆ What is the secret to prayer for you?

5

SISTER,
LET ME HEAR
YOUR VOICE

Will I be a voice in the wilderness?
Or will I simply live in the wilderness
seeking a voice?

—Anonymous

Contrary to popular belief, lies, and mistaken perceptions perpetuated by the media, the world is not filled with women who are living their best lives now.

Contrary to best-selling books, the talk show circuit, and the current set of razor thin supermodels, life does not always treat women well!

Contrary to the popular television show roster, the top ten "best" flicks, and the constant parade of "silly women" exposés reporting that there are women living full, productive, and fulfilling lives past sixty and seventy, in America and in every local congregation, there are women of all ages who are victims of domestic violence!

A crazy man (or series of crazy men!), an ungrateful child (or a group of ungrateful children!), and a demanding house (or several different homes!) is not the goal of every woman! There is life, satisfaction, and accomplishment beyond these highly touted and necessary roles for women. Many women have tested, tried, and pushed beyond the limits established by our society and culture.

Of course, there are any number of us who have accepted the man, borne the child, invested much energy in homes and yet found abundant life beyond these boundaries. While the rest of the world is coming out of the closet, demanding rights and acceptance, telling their stories and receiving an audience with every form of media, we who are mature, self-sufficient, and capable of choosing our own path, we who follow our own star and seek to live out our own divine purpose, we have also chosen to come out of our closets and to live out loud! We are claiming our voice! We will tell our truth!

The world is filled with secrets. We have been socialized to "be quiet," to "talk softly" and "be seen, not heard." Then there is the infamous line that declares, "What happens in this house stays in this house!" This phase has driven too many of us to become both dysfunctional and certifiably crazy. The time has come to speak. There will come a season, in each of our lives, when speaking truth, loudly, is demanded. There is a lost generation walking right behind us. They are wondering and confused about the direction for their lives. Keeping secrets will not help them at all.

We are a sandwich generation. Our daughters need to hear our real and honest truth. They have their skewed opinions of our lives, their selfish beliefs about our lives, and their rightful expectations of our lives. But their perceptions are not our realities. We were women way before we became their mothers. They need to know our truth.

Years ago, after watching the unfulfilled lives of our mothers, there were millions of us who decided not to follow their examples in the business of "mothering." We set our agendas toward other adventures and never looked back. Likewise, we have given birth to millions of babies, and, we have birthed other sorts of "babies" who continue to live, thrive, and prosper.

On the other side of the sandwich is those who are coming behind us. Many of us are now grandmothers and great aunts to a "now" generation—the generation who feels that they know it all. Their actions indicate that they don't know jack squat! They need an accurate accounting of our lives.

We are those women who have already made "her-story!" We are those women who have heard voices at midnight, seen distant stars in the daylight, received visions from beyond our time, and created masterpieces from leftovers and scraps. We are those daughters of divine destiny who, somehow and some way, broke through the glass ceiling, climbed out of the boundary box, and made a conscious, wise, and purpose-filled choice to live out loud. For the central question of every woman's life is: Will I be a person with voice who lives in the wilderness? Or, will I simply live in the wilderness seeking (or refusing to have) a voice?

It began with a simple plan for me to enjoy a group of local sisters and to celebrate the beginning of a new year. I sent invitations that arrived with their stacks of Christmas and Kwanzaa cards and read:

"Please join me in celebrating an 'I'm Still Here' Brunch.
Life has tried its best to kick us in the teeth; to snatch our joy;
to rob us of our sanity; sobriety and salvation this year.
But God has given us the victory! We're still here!
Bring your testimony of triumph and a dish to share on
the very first Saturday of the New Year at WomanSpace!"

It was on! Sisters came. Stories were shared. Lives were challenged. Wounds were healed. New hope was given. Many women decided to begin a new journey and to live out loud. For in the company of other women there is safety, sanctuary, and a serenity that allows for broken spirits to confess their pain. In a circle of supportive sisters, women can be assured of nurture, understanding, and comfort. For the issue of domestic violence is alive and well. Most of us have experienced it in one form or another.

To start of our time together, I gave testimony about a recent sermon given in my own local congregation. The anger was yet alive within me. The audacity of the male preacher to stand and to speak about domestic violence from the pulpit in a cavalier fashion had caused me to want to fight, to yell, and to scream. From my seat on the pulpit, I had said, "Don't tell that story! Don't go there!" But, the preacher continued despite my verbal complaints and my escalating pain.

Our pastor was out of town that Sunday and had invited a city official, who happens to be a Pentecostal pastor, to preach the Sunday message. He is a nice looking man. He has a very charismatic personality. He can surely make you laugh. And our congregation seemed to enjoy his preaching style. But on this Sunday he decided to talk about his low self-esteem issues and how it came from the abusive household in which he had been raised. I felt that he was off to a good start to let the secret out of the closet! I knew that he was going to address a primary issue in local congregations. The preacher told us that he was the youngest of his siblings and often stayed around his mom in the house. He told how his father was not a very nice man. He told us that he worked long hours and made good money but gave very little to his wife to take care of the house. He told us how his father would go to the restaurants and buy food for him and the dogs, while the rest of the family would go hungry. Then, he decided to tell the story of how one day his father beat his mother while he was at home.

It was here that I began to say, "Don't tell that story!" But he would not listen. He went on to tell us that his father got angry at something his mother said, went into the kitchen and got a black, cast iron skillet, and hit his mother in the head! I screamed again, "Stop." But he went on to tell us that he witnessed a bit of his mother's skull flying across the room! And as he went to tackle his father, it was then that his mother stood up to slap him, as she reminded him, "He's your father."

The preacher went on to say that his mother got a white cloth and some olive oil and put it on her bleeding head and never went to the doctor or to the emergency room for care. I sat there. I was angry, dismayed, and upset that he had not ended the story by telling us how God had struck his father dead! Instead he used this preaching occasion to tell us that despite his abusive household, he had found self-esteem and answered his call to ministry and to even go into politics.

He missed a prime opportunity to teach about domestic violence in the church. He missed a teaching moment to talk to church members and those attending about the sin of domestic violence. He blew it with me that day! Please know that I went to him immediately after worship to ask about the end of the family story. I went to ask him why he felt that it was alright to make this "pitch" for wife beating from the pulpit without saying anything to those in the pew who were guilty. All that he could say was that one day, years later, his father had died a miserable death. But, his mother stayed with him until he died. I walked away, sad and unfulfilled. I will never sit and listen to him preach again!

With my story of anger and pain, the doorway opened for others to share regarding the issue of domestic violence and the silence within their own local congregations. The truth is that we have all been complicit in the sin of domestic violence around us.

The truth is that every institution in our culture has taught us to be weak, sniveling, quiet women who will please and stand by our man. Institutions are self-perpetuating entities. They were all built to uphold the status quo of men in charge and women being their charges. Institutions don't change rapidly. Institutions don't change willingly. Institutions were never designed to uplift or to support women and their rights. Institutions will only change when we, women across the world, band together and begin to stand up and to take our God-given rights!

I am the victim of incest. This is an act of domestic violence. My mother denied knowing what was occurring in her home. This too is an act of domestic violence. The domestic violence became a mountain, a huge mountain in my life. None of the institutions in my childhood were prepared to hear my story. I was a child. I was "owned" by my parents. Their wills, their ways, and their craziness was allowed, permitted, and "sanctified" by the church! My father was ordained clergy! My mother was an active woman in the local church. The only option for me was to leave home. The week after my eighteenth birthday, I ran away from home.

There is no doubt in my mind that when mountains will not move, you can! God has given us the capacity to use our free wills. This is the time to select from the multiple options, selections, and choices within our world. Today, there are agencies, advocacy groups, and shelters in place to assist us. The goals for intervention within agencies that advocate for domestic violence victims are these: 1) safety for the victim and any children; 2) accountability of the victimizer; 3) restoration if possible; and, finally, 4) doing the grief work of mourning if the relationship is not one of reconciliation.

Reconciliation is not always the answer! Reconciliation requires a partner who is willing to be accountable, repentant, and ready to go to work on the issues that caused battering in the first place. No longer do informed counselors tell women to "go back and make it work." For this counsel has been the reason that many women are dead today. Violence escalates! Those who do violence have serious issues that require serious, whole-hearted, and committed work.

We with sight, voice, and foresight within the church must be the ones helping to create new norms and new values regarding the issue of domestic violence. We with call, compulsion, and compassion must now get busy raising our voices, teaching, and instructing that domestic violence is not acceptable in the sight of God. "We don't do that here! We don't act that way here!" These are the messages that many hurting, scared, and invisible women and children are aching to hear in the place that is called "a sanctuary."

Some years ago, I read of a group of Japanese women who got together and talked about the battery that they were experiencing. They developed a strategy that all could agree to carry out when called upon. The next time that a woman was being beaten, she got a pot and a wooden spoon and began to pound the pot as hard as she could. Her neighbors heard her and would get their pots and wooden spoons and run to the front of that woman's house. Other women decided to join forces. Soon there was a very embarrassed man being publicly shamed as a crowd of women stood outside of his home, beating on pots with wooden spoons. The issue of domestic violence decreased greatly. The women claimed their collective voice!

REFLECTIONS

- How would you describe yourself in regard to the issue of domestic violence? Are you in the wilderness seeking a voice? Or are you a voice in this vast wilderness?

- Is there a shelter for victims of domestic violence in your local area?

- Have you ever been bold enough to confront a sister that you felt was being abused? How did you seek to assist her?

- How is the matter of domestic violence being addressed in your local newspaper? What about in your community? What about in your local church?

- What books, articles, and resources can you lay your hands on if a domestic violence victim calls you for assistance or counsel?

6

SISTER, I FEEL THE KNIVES IN YOUR BACK

White culture not only has impeded
Black people's ability to embrace themselves,
but has also interfered with their ability
to know God.

— Kelly Brown Douglas

We live in a world where our back may be stabbed, our confidence betrayed, and our reputation maligned in a "New York minute." We live in a time when discouragement, disappointment, despair, and depression seem to be the bywords of our lives. We live in a nation where wrong is celebrated, where the negative is uplifted, and where put-downs are a way of life. We live in a world where injustice reigns, inhospitality is rampant, and all sorts of sexual depravity is practiced in the family of God. Yet, we also live in a world where our covenant-making and covenant-keeping God is alive, well, and ready to renew our failing trust, as we begin again by getting up and starting all over again.

Once upon a time there was a singing preacher who lived in the backwoods hill country of Ephraim. One day he took a woman from Bethlehem in Judah to be his wife. It is recorded in the nineteenth chapter of the book of Judges that this was in a time when there was no king, no God representative, in Israel. This couple got into an argument and she went home to Daddy, where she stayed for four months. Her husband finally decided to go and get her. So he traveled to her home and stayed there for five days. As the man, his wife, and a servant traveled home, they came into a town of the Benjaminites, who were also Jews. There an old Jewish man offered them hospitality.

When they had fed the animals and prepared for bed, a gang of local Jewish men, hell-raisers, surrounded the house demanding to sodomize the singing Levite! The old man offered both his virgin daughters and his concubine to this gang, saying, "Ravish them, and do whatever you want to them, but against this man do not do such a vile thing" (Judg. 19:24).

Male biblical interpreters say that the Middle Eastern rules of hospitality were so strong that the old man was forced to save the male guest in his house. Women were not considered worthy of being treated with hospitality, safeguarding, or being given value as human beings. Patriarchy established this "rule" of hospitality where a woman could be pushed out the door and gang raped all night long without any consideration. The rules of patriarchy have not been fully dismantled within the house of God!

The Bible says, "So the man seized his concubine, and put her out to them. They wantonly raped her, and abused her all through the night until the morning. . . . There was his concubine lying [dead] at the door of the house, with her hands on the threshold" (Judg. 19:25, 27). This is a horrible story of biblical domestic violence! I have never heard it preached from the pulpit. Have you?

This story is alive and well today. This story is not about long ago and far away. Across the nation, there are "brothers" who abuse their "sisters" in the name of manhood. I have experienced this lately and want to report that the pain of being raped continues to hurt hearts, destroy hope, and kill relationships! Yet, we are not alone. We are not dead and gone! We are alive and able to make some new decisions to speak out about the foolishness that has been allowed for too long.

The only thing necessary for old ways to continue is for you and for me to remain silent. I don't know about you, but, sister, I am speaking my way to wholeness! God created the entire world with words and then gave the gift to each one of us.

That singing preacher took his dead, raped, wife home on a donkey. Then he cut her up into twelve pieces and sent her body parts to every tribe in the nation. He commanded the men whom he sent saying, "Look at what 'they' have done to me!" And, the chapter concludes: "Has such a thing ever happened since the day that the Israelites came up from the land of Egypt until this day? Consider it, take counsel, and speak out."

This is a biblical mandate to each woman of God who has watched other women belittled, ignored, emotionally cut up, her self-esteem and competence sliced to pieces, and pushed aside. And it is a sure "Word" to each of us who has experienced it personally and tried to "nice" our way through!

The telling of this biblical story is another way to remind us that rape and other forms of domestic violence happen in God's name all over the country. The telling of this biblical tale of terror is simply another way of showing that women are yet thought of as human sacrifices when it comes to male authority in local congregations. The telling of this biblical horror story is my call for every woman to wake up, get up, and think about how many times you have experienced sexism and injustice in the church and then been expected to be quiet and compliant!

Something is really wrong! I believe that we are physically and mentally abused when we are expected to attend worship and perform the money-giving, money-raising, and kitchen duties of the ministry but cannot serve on official boards that count, spend, and control the money that we give and raise. I think that we are marginalized, reduced to menial tasks, and overlooked when we are refused entry into the pulpit ministries due to our gender. I sincerely feel that we are victims within God's house when we have no voice in the decisions that affect us, our families, community outreach, and our offerings—when all of the power lies within "the brotherhood." Women are in full leadership in organizations all across America, with the exception of God's church! Think about this. Reflect upon it. Talk it over with another sister. Then, do something or find another worship center!

All of us must come to a point in our lives when we stop complaining and start our own personal revolution! The FaithTrust

Institute has prepared a pamphlet entitled "What Every Congregation Needs to Know about Domestic Violence." This pamphlet explains that domestic violence refers to a pattern of violent and coercive behavior over another in an intimate relationship. It is not "marital conflict," "mutual abuse," "a lover's quarrel," or a "private family matter." It may consist of repeated, severe beatings, or more subtle forms of abuse, including threats and control. Statistics reflect that 95 percent of the victims are women who are very different from one another and just as varied in profession, religious backgrounds, and educational status. We cannot identify or profile a victim of domestic violence. Too often she stays in the abusive situation because of multiple fears.

I know the story of being afraid to leave God in the place where I worshipped. After giving so freely of myself to a group of sisters and "brothers," rape and sodomy was the last thing on my mind. I am naive! I am too trustful. For three years, I gave the best of my knowledge, experiences, and services to a particular congregation. When their senior pastor gave two weeks notice, I was there to "wipe weeping eyes" and hold down the fort! I was hopeful that the black church was maturing, changing, and being transformed by my ministry as a woman, a sister, and a pastor. But my "brothers" sold me out. First they took advantage of me with the petty monetary offering for visiting the sick, counseling, and doing two Bible study classes per week. I took their meager offering because I had been willing to do it for free! I felt it was my reasonable service!

I already had an office in the building and had been counseling and offering pastoral care for over two years. Taking on additional duties and getting paid for it felt like a move up and an acknowledgement that I was a faithful servant in the house of God. I got the opportunity to lead Sunday morning worship and to preach the first Sunday after our pastor vacated the pulpit. The deacons sought to find a male interim to come and preach every Sunday so that they could "look like a Baptist Church." I went along with their feelings, thinking that my professional behavior would win them.

Finally, the Search Committee was formed, announcements of applications went across America, and the deacons invited me to attend one of their meetings. Silly me went to the meeting thinking that they were going to pat me on the back! Silly me went thinking that they would tell me how grateful they were for my "over and above the call" of duty ministry. Silly me went hoping that they would ask more of me—which I was willing to do—while neglecting my own business at WomanSpace. I had asked Mista Chuck to attend the meeting with me and he replied, "They most likely have something good to say to you. You can go alone."

He was silly and naive too!

When I entered the deacons' meeting, which was already in progress, they asked me to come out of "their" pulpit and not offend anyone, especially not the new male interim pastor whom they were going to hire. They wanted me to continue to do all the things they had been paying me to do, while I was to quietly sit in the pew with my spouse and be silent! The devil is a lie!

Immediately, all of the women in ministry came to my mind. With a video snapshot of all the women whose backs I stand upon and the bridge that I am for other women and girls, I would not agree to this travesty. I asked if there were any "brothers" of integrity around the table. Honestly, I looked for just one! They *all* agreed with the chair of their board. I was the problem, the "loose cannon" and the reason that their church might split if I continued the pastoral work of the past three years. I and Grace (God's amazing grace) got up and walked out of their meeting, went over to my office, packed up all my belongings, and called Mista Chuck to come and take it and me home.

As I walked back into the meeting room and put the church keys on the table, I prophesized to each one of the little cowards that they would all feel my departure in the place of their male pride! For I am God's woman, God's messenger, and God's anointed servant whom they had already figuratively raped and tried to sodomize! Now they wanted to cut me into "pieces!" Big time payment is due each one of them! It's a covenant promise. It's a guaranteed covenant. It's a covenant signed in the precious blood of Jesus Christ!

The next Sunday, I put on a bright melon-colored St. John suit, some new shoes with plenty of sparkling rhinestones, and went to church, where I sat in the pew with my spouse. As the choir sang the invitation to prayer song, "speak to my heart, Lord Jesus, give me the words that will bring new life," my praying tears begin to roll. I got up and went to kneel at the altar with my hands upon the communion table.

There I began to weep and to wail. "Call for the wailing women. Let them come and take up lament for us as death has come into our windows," said the prophet Jeremiah (Jer. 9:20–21)! Every wail was a prayer. Every wail was a petition. Every wail was a speech about the injustice I had experienced in the house of God! God heard them all.

The ushers ran to attend me. Women came down from the choir. From every side of the sanctuary, women gathered around me. There was no need for me to have stood and made an announcement. They all knew that I had been put on "the chopping block" as I was sitting in the pew. None of them said a word to me. They simply surrounded me, put their hands on me, and prayed. I wailed and cried until my tears ended. I finally stood up and walked back to my seat, knowing that God cared about me and about the women who surrounded me, fully aware of the injustice that I had experienced in God's house.

> The suffering that you experience in being battered physically (spiritually) and psychologically is suffering that is put upon you against your will. It is involuntary suffering; you never chose it. It is the same kind of suffering as discovering that one has cancer because of exposure to a chemical dump or as the suffering of being injured by a drunk driver. You are harmed in some way because of someone else's negligence or cruelty—not because you chose to be harmed.[1]

I did not choose this pain!

Once again, a psalm helped renew my trust in God, along with my wailing prayer. "God, you're all I want in heaven and all I want on earth. When my skin sags and my bones get brittle, God is rock-firm and faithful. Look! Those who left God are falling apart! Deserters, they will never be heard from again! But, I'm in the presence of God—Oh, how refreshing it is! I've made God my home.

God, I'm telling the world what you do!" (Psa. 73:24–26 *The Message*). Claiming and reclaiming our voice gives us power, raises our self-esteem, and puts the world on notice that we will not go along in order to get along.

This is the type of covenant upon which I invite you to take a stand. This is not about some "reflection" that we will have forgotten before this time next month. We are in the beginning stages of realizing how insidious domestic violence is around us all. It is time that we each covenant to be who God has been calling and is calling us to be!

After experiencing the domestic violence of his own kinspeople, who sold him out to Herod and had him crucified by the Roman government, Jesus went to Calvary. He died, only to rise again! After resurrection, Jesus met Mary Magdalene in a garden and charged her to "go and to tell." We are all like Mary Magdalene, women of destiny and purpose! I refuse to be the mule, the donkey, or the silent, raped, sodomized, and cut-up woman—not this time! I wanted you to know that it happened to me, so I am telling!

We are on a continuing journey and only God knows where the roads will lead us. But, as we move, I invite you to grab hold of a covenant promise and hang in there! And tell it as you go! In your telling, you gain power. In your telling, you gain validation. In your telling, you help another sister to be freed to share her truth too.

The FaithTrust Institute pamplet concludes: "We can be helpful when an abusive situation is revealed by listening to the woman and believing her. We can tell her that she is not alone and that there is help available for her. Let her know that without intervention, abuse often escalates in frequency and severity. Help her to seek expert assistance and refer her to any specialized domestic violence counseling programs (not marital or couples counseling) that you know of locally. Help her to find a shelter, a safe house, or advocacy resources to offer protection for her and the children."

It is our continuing work to hold the abuser accountable. We cannot continue to minimize abusive behaviors. We can help batterers to seek specialized batterers' counseling to change their behavior; we can continue to hold them accountable and continue to support and protect the victim even after the batterer has begun a counseling program. If restoration of the relationship is to occur, it can only be considered after all these have taken place. As religious communities, our mandate is to minimize any roadblocks facing abused members of our congregations and to maximize the resources that exist within our religious traditions.

Be gracious to me, O Lord, for I am in distress;
my eye wastes away from grief,
my soul and body also. . . .
I have become like a broken vessel,
But I trust in you, O Lord;
I say, "You are my God" (Psa, 31:9, 12b, 14)

REFLECTIONS

♦ Have you ever experienced violence within your local congregation?

♦ Do you know of any other individual who has been subjected to domestic violence within your local congregation?

♦ How do women claim their "voice" within your local congregation?

♦ What does "silence" cover within your local congregation?

7

SISTER, GOD VALUES YOUR TEARS

The time came when to remain a bud was
more painful than to risk to blossom.

—Anais Nin

At my age, there are many things I cannot do. I cannot play tennis; however, it is wonderful to watch the awesome Williams sisters win crystal trophies in professional tennis competitions. But playing tennis is not my specialty.

At my age, there are many things I cannot do. It is a joy to have a young man who loves to swim living with me. Knowing my grandson Giraurd, he will make swimming an art, for he is an avid swimmer. On vacations, the hotel pools seem to just call his name. There are many famous swimmers. But swimming is not my specialty.

At my age, there are many things I cannot do. I cannot carry a tune. I am a preacher-teacher in the African American tradition. I come from a line of singing, whooping preachers. However, one year when I called my girlfriend, Dr. Janet Hopkins, and sang "*Happy Birthday*" to her answering machine, she called me back just to inform me that she loved me despite my nonsinging voice! For singing is not my specialty.

At my age, there are many things I cannot do. But I do have a specialty. Some folks would say that I specialize in talking because I do it so much and with such great passion. But talking is not my specialty either.

Many folks think I specialize in writing, since I seem to be perpetually working on a new book. Let me hurry to say that I see my writing for the sisterhood as a gift of encouragement and another extension of my teaching/preaching ministry. Writing, however, is not my specialty.

Many folks think I specialize in being a good mother. For we have raised three children, been fiscally responsible for Chuck's four children, and now are the legal guardians of Giraurd. But, if the truth were known, I don't really even like children around me for too long! Since I had them, a woman's gotta do what a woman's gotta do! But believe you me, kids are not my specialty.

Sisters, allow me to let you in on a secret. My specialty is tears. I really do know how to cry. I cry easily. I cry freely. I cry often. There are many times when I have wished that I were not such a crybaby. There was a time when I cried only when I was upset or angry. But the older I get, the better I can cry. One day after my son Grelon was diagnosed with end-stage kidney failure, I sat by a lake and I tried to cry as much water as there was lake. I really tried to cry out all my tears. But I have discovered that the older I get, the better I can cry. I tell you with no hesitation, at my age, I am a champion crier!

Like the women of Jeremiah's day, I understand the worth of my tears. Like God's people of old, I realize the value of my tears. Like the ancestors, I have come to grips with the fact that sometimes all you can do is cry. Crying is an honorable profession. When Jeremiah was prophet to Israel, women were employed as professional criers, weepers, and wailers. Crying became famous. It is recorded that even "Jesus wept."

There comes a time in the course of human events when tears are just plain necessary. Whether you are together, tough, or bad, life will present periods of difficulties and pain—times when you need to know how to cry. When you find yourself standing at the crossroads of disappointment and despair, it is no laughing matter. It is time for tears. Sister, when you arrive at the intersection of Sorrow Boulevard and Suffering Avenue, trying to figure out how to move and which direction to take, sometimes all you can do is sit down and cry.

The Book of Lamentations is an ode to Israel's crying time. As Jeremiah looked at the conditions all around him, all he could do was cry. Like them, we too need a World Crying Day! For there is no place on God's inhabited universe where pain is not great. There is no inhabited spot without violence or where human loss is bearable. There is no area where destruction of relationships and the decay of dreams and hopes within mass urban devastation has not become a way of life. When we look at our world, when we see the killing of our children all across the world, and as we watch the continuing moral, social, cultural, and religious collapse of values all around the world, we need to gather as sisters and weep, wail, mourn, and cry!

Jeremiah, famous for his personal tears, looked at the people of God, caught between the Exodus and the Exile, and wrote a funeral dirge, a lament of pain, and a grief-stricken wail about Israel's lack of faithfulness to a faithful God. Israel kept repeating a perpetual cycle of forgetfulness, internal destruction, and pleading whines to God, who desired instead confession and repentance. Israel's mission was tarnished. Their light to the nations was not twinkling very brightly. Their ability to survive was in question. So, as Jeremiah wrote Lamentations after the fall of Jerusalem, it was with a heavy heart. Everyone of us is familiar with a heavy heart. We have often stood in his shoes.

Jeremiah stood looking at the people of God and scripted a symphony of pain. Tears fell on every page. Those tears were the voices that reached beyond mere words, as our tears are the prayers that God hears when our ability to speak is absent. God reads every teardrop! My Granny used to tell me that God can interpret even our moans and our groans. Grief gives us no choice but to allow our tears to flow in order that hope might be restored as our burdens are shared with a listening, caring, and healing God.

Lamentations declares that Israel's wounds are great, the pain is real, and the people have great cause for genuine concern. Yet, Jeremiah longs to break Israel out of their crying cycle. He finds a simple method for coming up out of the hole of depression. He designs a strategy guaranteed to move the heart of God. Jeremiah begins to pray with his tears. (Go! Light a candle. Get into your rocking chair. Hush your mouth and cry!)

Jeremiah says, "The thought of my affliction and my homelessness is wormwood and gall! My soul continually thinks of it and is bowed down within me. But this I call to mind, and therefore I have hope: The steadfast love of the Lord never ceases, his mercies never come to an end; they are new every morning; great is your faithfulness. 'The Lord is my portion,' says my soul, 'therefore I will hope in him'" (Lam. 3:19–24). The gift of memory is often an antidote for our tears.

When we can cry due to a burdened spirit, we do it because crying is a silent form of prayer. Tears are our unspoken petitions for God to come and intervene on our behalf. Tears are our inarticulate and inaudible pleas to the only help we know. God understands and answers speechless tears. This is one of the reasons that I specialize in tears! For tears of prayer put us in touch with Jesus Christ. Prayer gives us access to the Ancient of Days. Prayer connects us with the Comforter of Israel. Want to be effective in your efforts of moving us forward from this current valley of world lethargy and universal despair? Well, become one of Jeremiah's band of weeping and wailing women! Learn what many sisters already know, and that's how to cry over the needs of others. Our tears of compassion are prayers that God hears, understands, and answers.

Yes! I specialize in tears. But they are not tears of hopelessness. My tears are not from faithlessness. For I recall God's faithfulness in other time periods. So my tears are prayers to a right now God! My tears empty out emotions that crowd my spirit, mess with my mind, and keep me stuck in one place—not being able to respond to God's call to move forward. My tears move me to act on behalf of those things I am crying about.

We cannot just sit and cry. But we do have to cry as well as cooperate with the Mover and Shaker of the universe. The world needs our tears. The nation needs our tears. The cities need our tears. Families need our tears. The church needs our tears. Our tears say that we care about the issues in the world. Our tears say that our hearts are moved with compassion and that we are willing to get up and do what we can in order to make a difference in our world.

As we cry, in order to make tomorrow better, it is essential to recall the pain and hurt that brings the tears, and to look forward to see what ministry-work God is assigning us to do. An African proverb says "It's a wise one who plants a tree that will never give that one shade." We have many things over which we need to cry. Three of the biggest issues that need our tears today are the continued racism and sexism in the world's culture and the domestic violence within the church. As "nice" women, these are huge agenda items, which we like to avoid talking about and taking action on. But we have to do more than sit, wring our hands, and cry. It is time to cry. And then it is time to continue to work toward eradicating all violence, especially toward women and children.

We can cry over the conditions of our sisters and their babies who are having babies. But, will you take your cute self to the barrio? to the ghetto? or to Appalachia? Would you make the decision to volunteer in the projects and teach children how to lift themselves up and help them learn skills for employment?

We can cry over domestic abuse and gang violence in our communities. But will you give a testimony about how you left your abusive situation and then offered to volunteer at the shelters in your community?

We can cry over the plight of so-called Third Word nations and the refugee camps shown on every news channel. But what are you willing to do to help the struggling immigrants in your own city? What about the Third World women who are yet undergoing genital mutilation?

We can cry over the loss of our youth in drive-by shootings. But are you a tutor or mentor who works in an after-school or Saturday program making a difference to one child? Have you volunteered to mentor a young woman who wants a change in her life after having a baby out of wedlock?

We can cry over the breakup of marriages and the number of folks who are cohabitating without marriage or committed relationships in order to have loving relationships. But will you work more diligently to be nice to the spouse and significant other that you have now? Will you reach out to other single women and become a supportive community to those whose pain you can read behind their smiling mask?

We need to cry over the plight of women everywhere! But will you honestly go to work on the needs of the hurting, depressed, and grieving woman who lives inside of you?

We need to cry. But we also need to continue our labors in spite of our tears. For perseverance while crying is mandated. A tough spirit and a can-do attitude is essential. We can cry and push past set limitations. A new perspective on tears is required. Cry and mow down the best arguments others will use to persuade you to cease and desist. For an "eye on the prize" mindset is what God is demanding from each one of us.

God does collect our tears. God also expects us to work. God honors our tears. God also demands our wholehearted response to the situations in the world that we can affect. Around the whole world there are problems. Pain causes all of us to cry. Our tears can be those of self-pity, which will keep us stuck in the same place. Or those same tears can assist us in cleansing our tired eyes, seeing a new vision, and then, with purpose and clarity and determination, moving ahead to new life and brand new starts.

Our days of being stuck, simply sitting and crying, have to come to a halt. We must become like Jesus, who did weep, and after he dried his weeping eyes, he still looked death and destruction in the face and called Lazarus to get up and come forth! In a graveyard, Jesus sent two weeping sisters and their resurrected brother on the move toward a brand new future. Their tears did not keep them stuck in one place.

The book of Lamentations was not the end of the story for God's people! Many are the books of history that followed. The blank pages of world history are yet awaiting our decision and our response. Girlfriend, what will you do? I suggest that you cry and move. My sister, cry and move! Remember, I am on the crying and moving journey with you. For, sister, you need to cry and you need to save yourself!

REFLECTIONS

- ◆ What do you know about the power in lamenting?
- ◆ What makes you cry?
- ◆ When was the last time that you felt that your tears were actually your prayers?
- ◆ What did you learn new about tears/crying/lamenting?

8

SISTER,
THERE IS
POWER IN A
SAFE TOUCH

*There is a long macho tradition in
this culture that pronounces certain kinds
of violence as perfectly appropriate.*

—Sarah J. McCarthy

I read the book *Lightning* by Danielle Steele, who is one of my favorite authors. It is the story of a beautiful, successful female attorney and a good-looking, successful man who fall in love, get married, and have a wonderful relationship. Because they were both middle-aged when they met, they were constantly touching one another with affection and with care. They were married well over fifteen years when the wife became pregnant. They had a daughter who looked just like her mommy and the couple felt that life was complete. Then lightning struck!

Following a routine mammogram, a deep mass was found that necessitated the removal of one of the woman's breasts. A modified radical mastectomy had to be performed. Then she had to undergo six months of chemotherapy. She began a regiment of sickness, violent vomiting, and fatigue. She spent many days with her face laying on the bathroom floor, too weak to make it into either her bedroom or her office as she tried to retain a sense of normalcy in her life.

She longed for her husband's touch. She longed for his comfort and tenderness. She screamed at him to stand with her, to offer her the care and the support that she had grown so accustomed to receiving. But he could not provide it. He would not. He did not. As he looked at his wife and the place where her breast had been "sliced" off, it scared him. Her bald head, without a wig, disgusted him. He was afraid that she was going to die and leave him. So he would not reach out to touch her. Instead, he began to reach out to someone else. This was, in a sense, an act of psychological sexual violence!

Human touch is so essential to each one of us. Touch is a God-given gift. Human touch is so effective, which is why the church continues to do "laying on of hands" in different worship services. Human touch is so extraordinary in its ability to communicate so many human emotions. Touch can say, "I care." Touch can say, "I am with you." Touch can say, "It is going to be alright." Touch can say, "You are not alone." However, Danielle must know from experience, because she writes about this need so well, that human, caring touch is not always available when we need it most! The only safe touch that we can daily rely on is a touch from the Divine.

> Through his body Jesus was able to interact in the world and to enter into relationship with others. Moreover, that Jesus touched, healed, and raised the dead indicates his own respect for the bodies of others. The body can be a vehicle for divine presence and the means by which human beings can communicate agape. The body is the physicality of sexuality, that which signals the potential for one to be authentically human and hence to reflect the image of God in the world . . .[1]

Thank God for the divine touch of Jesus Christ, who, through the body ministry, is alive and well in the church.

The book of Mark, chapter 5, gives us a clear portrait of Jesus, who had been run out of town for touching and healing a man of color who was living in a graveyard. It is obvious that this man needed a divine touch; he was uneducated, unemployed, and not caring for his family. His hair was wild and uncombed. His clothes were torn and disarrayed. His speech was unintelligible. He had made his home in a graveyard. So Jesus left a big crowd of arguing church folks and went to heal this desperate and sick man. It was all that the man needed. The demons that had held him were forced into a herd of swine that ran into the waters and drowned. The townspeople were not very happy that the pigs had destroyed themselves. Therefore, they politely asked Jesus to leave.

The healed man wanted to travel with Jesus, who had so effectively touched him. But Jesus told him to return home and be a witness to the powerful effect of touch. We are not given any details as to how the man then got clothes or a comb for his wild hair. But we are given sufficient information to allow us to know that at the end of his "touch session" with Jesus, he was both "clothed and in his right mind." This story lets me know that often, when we feel so far from any help, so out of touch with our community, and so alone, Jesus will just happen by our way. With only one correct, proper, and healing touch, restoration can be ours.

At the request of those townspeople (Mark 5:17), Jesus set off for another place. The crowd grew, for people always want to be part of a spectacular event. The throng was trying their best to get as close as they could to this "miracle worker." As Jesus moved forward, there was a woman in the crowd who certainly had no business being there. She was a needy woman who had been ill for more than twelve years. She was bleeding and therefore had been labeled by her community as "unclean." She was to be confined to her quarters. She was to remain away from others so as to not contaminate them. Certainly she was not to be in the congregation of a rabbi or any temple leader. If she would touch any man, even by accident, it would render him ritually impure, and there were many series of cleansing rites that he would have to undergo before resuming services. Nevertheless, this bodacious woman was in the crowd with a determination to touch the hem of the garment that Jesus was wearing.

It is so much like life that there should be a man outside of community who needed a touch and a woman who had been forced outside of community who was seeking a touch. This is another story of spiritual abuse, or what we might call domestic violence within God's "house!" This story enfolds all of us. Like the man in the graveyard, we may be in need of someone to reach out to us, or, like the bleeding woman, we may be the one reaching out for help.

There are days when I call God just for myself, for my burdens, for my needs, and for my issues. Then there are those days when I am reaching after God on behalf of others who I know have burdens, needs, and issues that they are trying so diligently to hide. This is the awesome privilege of being a child of God. The gift of discernment is operating in the church. Even when I try to hide my needs—when I would rather sit in my graveyard alone, when I think that I can fool all the people, all the time, with my pretend smiling face—there is someone God will send my way to touch me.

This is a God wink! This is that moment when the intersection between what I need and what another can provide lets me know that God is watching, caring, and intervening on my behalf. At the right time, even in the wrong place, God will find us, seek us out like the man in the graveyard, and touch us with divine love. Or we can be like this bold woman and get out in the community to discover the touch that we need to survive and to experience abundant life.

This woman, our sister, had spent all of her resources trying to find help. The doctors could not diagnose her condition. The home remedies had not helped. The wisdom of the women's quarters had not stopped the flow of blood. She was at a point of desperation. She was at the place where she did not care about the rules, the traditions, or even the consequences. Girlfriend knew that if she did not find a cure that she was going to die. So she went to seek the One with the right touch, baby!

Dignity flies out the window when you are desperate. Pride takes a hike when all the correct procedures have failed you. Social correctness and political savvy meant absolutely nothing to this woman who needed a divine touch. So, down on her knees, in the middle of the crowd, she crawled just to touch the hem of the fringes on Jesus' robe. She got the right touch that she needed. She was not spotted. She was not called out. Nor was she seen by the crowd. Jesus, however, realizing that healing touch had left him, turned around and cried out, "Who touched me?" Well, folks thought that he had lost his mind. The crowd was so dense. The people were pressing in on each other. They were a mass of confusion. But Jesus knew that someone seeking a divine touch had just received it.

Getting the right touch and receiving safe touch is all about our personal determination. It is about putting our faith in motion. It is about our commitment to live fully and wholly. It is about our personal deep-seated desire and intention to be better, to experience more, and to move to the next level. It was this desire that had this woman crawling in the crowd. She recognized that she could have been stoned to death for breaking the laws of purity. She understood that she could have been completely banned from the community, for her presence had made each man there "unclean." But she was also clear that this was her last chance, her final hope, her most immediate opportunity to get assistance. She dared to risk what life she had left. She took a giant leap of faith and gambled that tomorrow would be better than today. And she got the right, safe touch that she needed!

When she stepped up to confess that she had touched him, Jesus said to her, "Daughter, your faith has made you whole." She had a new lease on life. She had a new possibility for living. She had hope that she would be better than she had been for the past twelve years. Her gambling paid off. Her disobedience to the rules of the church got her just what she needed. Her vulnerability became her blessing as the touch of Jesus gave her healing.

We are each affected in some way by the declining economy, the old guard gatekeepers, by new positions, financial stress, strained family relationships. or personal challenges. We might choose to ignore or deny the issues or live on our independent Fantasy Island! Jesus can find us on our isle of "do nothing." The story of our graveyard brother proves that. But, on the other hand, I am more inclined to be like that creeping, crawling, and seeking sister who got out and got the healing touch that she needed.

That critical, life-giving touch transformed her, renewed her, set her free, and encouraged her broken spirit to soar again. I wish for each one of us that kind of touch. I pray that the Holy Spirit meets us at our point of need, breathes on us, pours into us, and washes over us with new life and fresh starts. That is the good news about these two stories: both the male and the female were able to start all over again. For our God is the God of many chances for new ideas, new goals, and new desires in our life. Regardless of our situation or circumstance, it ain't over yet!

The word for this day is "touch," the right touch: a safe touch and a healing touch. Whether you need a gentle, soothing, caring touch; an inclusive, quieting, and enabling touch; or have experienced a harsh, abusive, or limiting touch, there is space for you. All of us have a touch history. Each one of us can recover memories of different touches in our lives. There have been pats on the back that said, "You are good." There have been swats on the backsides that said, "You are not good." We've experienced touches as glances with the eyes that say, "I acknowledge you." And there have been glares from those same eyes that proclaimed, "I am gonna get you."

As children, too many of us have been victims of lustful, fawning, and inappropriate touch. This leaves too many of us yearning for an intimate touch and a healing touch from safe people in safe spaces.

At some point along our journey, lighting has struck each one of us and we have been forever changed. Today is our time to assure the little girl within us that we will only allow safe and healing touch from this day forward. We will only gather in sacred spaces. We will only touch others with our love. We will touch others with our caring prayers. We will touch others with our healing words, our calming exchanges, and the rituals that promote a healing community for all. We are women who can become sisters if we simply open ourselves to the presence of the Healing Christ. The good news is that there is no spot that God is not! And, in the company of our sisters and our God, we can reach out to hug. We can reach out to be hugged. The healing touch of our hands is the instrument that Jesus needs today. We need to help others experience God's anointing power, to be the balm that helps to erase the damage of wrong touches over the years.

Yes! This is a call for *you* and for *your* local congregation, local groups of women and local community groups to begin the practice of asking for and giving hugs. And don't go around acting as if you only *give* hugs. Be willing, be open, be vulnerable and confess the days, the times, and the occasions when you *need* a hug just for you.

The hands of women rock the cradles of the earth. Domestic violence demands that we use these same hands to rock each other into wholeness, healing, and healthy, life-giving relationships. I cannot ask the grocery store check-out clerk for a hug. I cannot ask the woman who is selling me a business suit, a purse, or a new pair of shoes for a hug.

But, in the company of my sisters, when my heart has been broken, when my spirit is thirsty for love, and my search over a dry and barren land has left me withered and crippled, I can come to my sisters, confess my need, and be hugged, held, and helped to live a while longer! Good hugs are healing. I need one right now. What about you?

REFLECTIONS

- What is your touch history?
- How do you respond today to an inappropriate touch?
- Are you in a safe congregation, a loving relationship where your touch needs are being met?
- What is your family history regarding hugging, touching, and reaching out in love?
- In what manner do you get your touch quota filled?

9

SISTER,
WE ARE ON
A JOURNEY

The Spirit of the Lord is upon me,
because the Lord has anointed me to
bring the good news…!

—Isaiah 61:1

Once upon a time a little Negro girl was born in the state of Alabama. She was born into a large family with a father and mother and many siblings. She was born into a struggling family where it was a challenge to be fed, clothed, loved sufficiently, supported adequately, and encouraged on a daily basis. Hers was an experience of emotional and physical abuse too many times. Although born into a religious family where the God of Abraham, Sarah, Isaac, and Rebecca were household topics, verbal, emotional, and physical abuse were often her lot.

She was named officially DaisyBelle. Implied in this name is floral beauty and a nature that would attract others. But families don't always use our given names, and this little girl was called Red by her siblings. Red was rough and she was tough. Red would argue and Red would fight. Red loved her family and she sought love in return. But, in this large family, Red had an inner hunger that was never satisfied. For you must understand that, even before Red was born, the Spirit of the Lord was upon her.

The Spirit of the Lord brings favor. The Spirit of the Lord brings a restlessness. The Spirit of the Lord brings a searching, seeking, and inquisitive mind. And, the Spirit of the Lord sets those who are chosen for ordained ministry on a journey that will lead them into unknown directions. The Spirit of the Lord is creative, imaginative, and far reaching. The Spirit of the Lord is gentle, but firm. The Spirit of the Lord is kind, but it is exacting and demands excellence. The Spirit of the Lord is peaceful, but it is also frustrating to those who don't quite understand what is going on at the time.

Before her birth, the beautiful flower, DaisyBelle, was chosen, consecrated, and commandeered for the ministry of God. She recognized that she was different. But this reality of being different didn't bring with it a blessed assurance. Her family simply thought that she was a difficult personality. But God always has a witness to the active presence of the Spirit of the Lord. And the preacher-woman, counselor, advocate, or therapist who can best assist other sisters with deliverance from any sort of domestic violence is one who has had some personal experience to work on in her life.

An Alabama school principal took a kind liking to Red. This woman of discernment began to spend time with this feisty little sister. She allowed Red access to her home. Greater yet, she allowed Red access into her heart, which begin a healing of the girl's inner pains and emptiness from emotional neglect and abuse. It is truth that it takes a village to raise a child. It is required of the whole Christian community to assist individuals on the journey toward full anointing of the Spirit of the Lord. Even though the principal was outside of Daisy's familiar circle, she began to invest in and cultivating her heart, mind, and spirit for something different, something better.

DaisyBelle's journey to her anointing began before her birth. Each one of us is called before our conception to do something that only we can accomplish upon the earth, in our time and in our place. Daisy's anointing grew in her family home, as she walked in the farming footprints of her preaching father, listened to the faith of her praying mother, and wrestled for her place among the siblings. Her annointing was stirred, fanned, and cultivated in the public school system of one of the most segregated states in America. For DaisyBelle was God's Beautiful Flower. And, God's daisies are hearty plants who annually are renewed and sustained.

"Famousity"—which means the daring to become bold, bodacious, out of the box, transformed, different, and famous—was spoken into DaisyBelle's life and spirit. This a word that we all need to know. "Famousity" is within each one of us, for we all have God's favor! The fragrance of DaisyBelle has touched you now, and its attraction will pull you along the way. You cannot hear about God's Beautiful Flower, DaisyBelle, without being changed. Famousity. Be on the alert for it!

A public school employee, a lowly paid instructor in the segregated, rural area of Aliceville, Alabama, became God's prophet to Red. She looked at DaisyBelle—who was filled with anger that she could not explain, stayed in trouble both at home and at school, fighting for what she thought were her rights—and this public servant declared to Red, "Famousity is in you!" Remember, what we see practiced and role modeled within our homes of origin will become our outward behaviors too, as was so with DaisyBelle.

What this older adult woman was trying to say to God's Beautiful Flower was this: The Spirit of the Lord is upon you. You have been called to preach the good news of Jesus Christ to the poor in spirit. Red, you have been anointed by God to heal the brokenhearted you come in touch with along your journey. You have been sent to announce freedom, liberty, and a second chance to every captive to sin, pardon to every prisoner sitting in places where they have confined themselves. God has chosen you, Beautiful Flower, to announce, to proclaim, and to teach that this is the year of God's amazing grace. Red, you have been chosen to tell the world that we can celebrate God's destruction of all of our enemies. You are going to offer comforting words to everyone who grieves and who mourns. DaisyBelle, on your journey, you are going to care for the people of Zion. You are going to give them bouquets of daisies instead of the ashes that they expect. It is your responsibility to present messages of joy, in sermons, in song, in drama, by your life, that contradict the world's messages of doom. Wherever you go, DaisyBelle, you will give people praising hearts in place of the brokenness that they carry. Beautiful Flower, it is required of you to rename God's people Oaks of Righteousness. As you journey, tell them that they have been planted where they are by God to display God's glory and to rebuild for the honor of God.

When the prophet principal spoke the word "famousity" into her spirit, Red didn't understand, had no idea what this adult was saying. Yet that word penetrated her very being and she began to walk differently, to expect more, to expand her horizons, and to set her sights on the far country. With God's help fueled by the Holy Spirit, with a loving community and self-determination, we can be healed of emotional spiritual, mental, physical, and verbal damage, both that which was intended and that which just happened. What happens in our childhood homes sets the stage for the ways that we will look for, anticipate, and expect to be treated all through our lives if there is no divine-human intervention. Thank God for the principal who entered Daisy's life.

The journey to an anointing takes God's servants to places where they will learn more to bring back home. The journey to an anointing requires an enlarging of the heart so that all types of persons may be respected and loved. The journey to an anointing demands that there is study, learning, digging, and even unlearning many of the lessons of our past in order to be approved by the world, as well as by the church. The journey to an anointing often sets us apart, makes us lonely, and keeps us guessing and confused. For God is Mystery and nothing with God is ever easy, clear, or cheap.

Beautiful flowers who grow annually must have deep roots. They need dirt and nutrients, and they are often severely cut back so that they will grow to their fullest potential. It is not always fun being a beautiful flower for God. But God requires us to grow, remain steadfast, and keep on keeping on . . . *because the Spirit of the Lord is upon us.*

One weekend, people assembled from all across the country to celebrate this fact. It was our privilege to say, "DaisyBelle, we too see the anointing that the principal called famousity. It was our prayer that one day you would see yourself as we saw you . . . a beautiful flower, gifted, consecrated, committed, and qualified for the role of servant of the Most High God. It was our prayer that your ministry would bring you back to you home state, in the city of Wetumpka. To God be all the glory!"

The radicality of God's love expressed in Jesus Christ means that God loves our very bodies . . . in order to respect the bodies and lives of others, we must first respect and love our own bodies and lives. Without self-acceptance, any acceptance of others is virtually impossible. Self-love is the absolute first step to loving others. And, ultimately, if we cannot love others, then we cannot fully love God, as our love for God is manifest through our love of others. In the words of Karen Baker-Fletcher, loving ourselves is the "first order of business" to loving God. The summary of the law referred to in the Bible is like this: "You shall love the Lord your God with all your heart, all your soul, and all your mind. You shall love your neighbor as yourself." This commandment clearly shows the interrelatedness of self-love and the love of others, as well as the need to love God with all that we are as human beings.[1]

This is a story of an emotional healing that is yet in active process! For DaisyBelle graduated from college with a degree in elementary school education, earned a master's degree in psychology and another master's in divinity, and taught school for twenty-two years. All along her journey she has worked at becoming her best self. She struggled, was challenged, and survived her family dysfunction, intentionally! She has sought council, gone for help, admitted her need for healing, and made herself available to learning new patterns for growth and development.

At the ripe age of forty, Daisy allowed wholesome love into her life. She got married to a good friend, Nelson Quiney, in a huge and lovely wedding ceremony. She finally became an ordained minister in the denomination of her childhood. Family and friends came to be with her as she began another new journey, following in the footsteps of her dad, but without his emotional hang-ups to hold her down! She was called to pastor a local congregation in her home state. She returned to help right the wrongs that she had experienced as a young child. The journey of anointing is not for any one individual; it is for the full body of Christ. Now it is time for her to help heal those who sit in the pews and those who come damaged from their homes. Thank God that this cycle of healing continues!

WOMEN AND PREACHING

Who is a faithful woman preacher?

One who is engaged in hearing her own voice and acknowledging the voices of others;

one who dares to use her voice in dialogue with God, with the church, and in the world;

one who is constantly engaged in retrieving the voices of women from the past and in this present world;

one who consistently lives in the full realization that God has given women gifts, resources, voices, and power to make a difference in the world;

one who is suspicious of self-denial; she knows her power and from where her authority stems;

one who risks believing that God does not want her to mute her voice;

one who struggles to find and to use the voices of other women;

one who is willing to listen to the voices of others without intimidation;

one who honors every voice, not avoiding conflict or anger, but hearing and accepting difference;

one who faces the differences and realizes that truth cannot be voiced without risk to loosing some relationships;

one who treads the dangerous and lonely ground of trusting her voice even when the community doesn't want to hear;

one who is committed to not give in to the comfort of silence;

one who is willing to allow her story to be told in her messages of hope;

one who is willing to use her life experiences as illustrations to show God at work;

one who will not compromise the gospel of Jesus Christ even at risk to her reputation and livelihood;

one who will advocate for the justice of every sister!

This is a godly woman and her own works will praise her in the gates! (Prov. 31).

REFLECTIONS

- ♦ What does the term "anointing" mean to you?
- ♦ Have you come to understand the "famousity" that is within yourself?
- ♦ Who first spotted that you were special and significant outside of your family?
- ♦ What is your family of origin's lack or deficit that has caused you the most struggles as an adult?
- ♦ What did you learn that will help you along the way?

10

SISTER, EVERY SYSTEM CAUSES PAIN AND SUFFERING

*Within the church, women have been
more apt to polish the brass, arrange the
flowers, put cookies on a plate, clean up,
keep the nursery, be led, pass the credit,
look pretty, and be supportive. In other
words, women have frequently functioned
more as church handmaids than religious
meaning makers or symbol creators.*

—Sue Monk Kidd,
  The Dance of the Dissident Daughter

*Systems: A group of interacting bodies
under the influence of related forces . . .
serving a common purpose.*

— *Merriam-Webster's Collegiate Dictionary*

Hello Sista Linda,
    I pray all is well with you. I just wanted to let you know
that I am back home now, in Florida, and so glad to be here.
Before I left the church in Virginia, the pastor confessed that
everything I had said about his sexual and spiritual abuse
toward me was the truth! Can you believe it! He finally confessed after all of his attempts to defame me! And he told
his congregation that he is a liar and a hypocrite, that he

has been faking ministry for fourteen years, empty, and that he had nothing for them! He has five members left now, which are the only other people who moved with us to Virginia from Atlanta.

Several other issues have been exposed at our "sending church" as well. Today, I received a call from my friend, Sara, VP of the Hope of Survivors Ministry. She had received a call from a young lady at our "sending church" who is pregnant from one of the leading songwriters and praise leaders in the country! The church is attacking her! The bishop told her that he was going to pay for her medical expenses and take care of her and her baby. He told her not to get an attorney and provided counseling for her through pastoral care. Then he turned right around and his attorney served her papers. The bishop has not given her anything and the elder told her to get on public assistance. She moved from New Orleans for the elder and this is her second pregnancy (she had an abortion the first time), and both he and the bishop are saying that she is psychotic, on drugs, sick, and needs help! They are saying that she seduced him and this only happened one time, and that she has suffered with bouts of depression (sound familiar?). But she told me that this is a two-year relationship. They are saying that she is trying to attack his ministry and his family. She was working for him on his last CD as his project manager and she has not received any money from him. She has a lawyer now and the elder has a lawyer. Her lawyer is currently trying to contact the local newspaper to expose this situation. This has also happened with several other women at the "sending church" and they are attacking those women as well.

She told me that a friend of hers directed her to my article on the website, and our experiences are very similar. Right now, she is employed during temp work for a legal firm, she is about to lose her home, and you know that she does not have a lot of money saved for medical care or food. I told her that she did not need to talk to anyone from

*the "sending church" and to seek counsel outside of their
affiliations. They told her that it would be ungodly to take
legal action and go to the media. But she has a baby on
the way and they are really persecuting her.*

*She needs to talk with someone. I told her that she
can contact me any time. I would like for you to minister to
her and I'm sending her your e-mail address. Bishop has
asked her for the e-mails that she and the elder have been
exchanging with each other. And now Bishop is saying that
she is trying to extort him. She has over 500 e-mails over
the course of their relationship. I have decided to help her
as much as I can. She asked me if I would speak with her
about my experiences, and although I want to move on with
my life, I feel the need to help her in any way.*

*Just wanted to let you know what's been going on.
I know that you told me to leave it behind and move on with
my life. I had every intention of doing that and then I got
this call today. I pray all is well with you, and please keep
me in your prayers.*

*Sincerely,
Your Sister*

How I wish that this was fictitious, a made-up letter to help with
the flow of this book! How I wish that we really didn't have to know
that there are men in God's church who continue to perpetrate
harm against women who come to the church to serve and to assist
in ministry. How I wish that all of us were saved, safe, sanctified,
and set apart to do authentic, honest, and spiritual ministry in the
name of God. But wishing does not make it so. The letter is an actual one from a sister-friend of mine who has her own pain-filled
history that called another sister to seek her out for help.

When I went to teach a United Methodist Regional School of
Christian Mission on the topic "Children and the Bible," also the
title of a book that I helped to write, I discovered another painful
reality about God's church. At our opening discussion around the
boardroom table, all of the leadership was discussing the opening

plenary and how the Bible story of Tamar, the raped daughter of King David, would be handled. The issue at hand was "how do we make it presentable to the audience?" I had a fit! I had an epiphany! I had a divine revelation! I opened wide my mouth to establish just why God has sent me all the way across the country to be present at this particular time in history.

The story of King David's rape of Bathsheba and the subsequent curse against his family by God shows us just how serious God takes the issue of domestic abuse. In the church, we don't want to say that David "raped" Bathsheba. We want to make it sound nice, holy, and pious. "He had relations with her." NOT! He looked out his palace window; he saw a lovely woman bathing after her monthly period; he lusted after her and sent his guards to fetch her to him for sex! This was not an "affair." This was not consensual sex. This was a king forcing a subject to consent. This is called rape! Then he had her spouse killed so he could keep her as a wife (one of several). God placed a curse against David's family success.

David's family became divided. The son of one wife, Anmon, raped Tamar, the daughter of another of David's wives. He plotted. He planned. He schemed and acted out a wicked, ugly, and nasty role to get Tamar into his bedroom. Then after he raped her, he loathed her and threw her out of his house and had the door bolted! Her story ends: "So Tamar remained, a desolate woman, in her brother Absalom's house" (2 Sam. 13:20b). The rape was the end of her life's story. The rape stole her future. The rape made her a victim. It was kept quiet. Yet these women wanted to paint a "presentable" picture about Tamar's rape!

We need to get a clue about the power of systems. Our government is divided into three distinct systems: executive, judicial, and legislative. Our levels of government are federal (national), state, and local. Our bodies' digestive systems are comprised of systems: intake, digestive, and elimination. The universal church is sectioned too: the world church, various demoninations, and local bodies of believers. And we subdivide the local church into the building, the people, and the priest/pastor.

In a functional system, all parts work in unity for the good of the whole. The family is a system: The family of origin (mother, father, siblings), and the extended family (grandparents, in-laws, and other relatives, some blood and some not). In a functional system, all parts work in unity for the good of the whole; however, not all systems are functional. There can be dysfunction at every level. This includes the church of the Living God!

Every system is composed of subsystems: a group of related forces helping to maintain the whole. Systems are designed to reinvent themselves or to self-perpetuate. Systems have an organized set of principles, doctrines, rules, and ideas to maintain their organization. Because of this, systems have a tendency to become oppressive and cause suffering to the little ones, the lesser parts, which can tend to become insignificant and invisible to the whole.

One of the greatest problems with any system is that of the relationship of the single individual to the whole or greater system. People align themselves with certain parts of the system in order to survive and to grow more powerful.

For example , our country is at war with Iraq. Soldiers cease to be "people" and become numbers assigned to a subsystem in order to make the entire system more effective. When this occurs, all "people" become expendable, no more than items that add to the statistical data that is gathered to support the greater system.

One of the things that we have to come to grips with about this particular war and the "war" within the church is that all parties feel that they are working on behalf of God! The people in Iraq are not divided in their minds or spirits about for whom they are at war. They live and they die for Allah/God! They have no tendency to subdivide into the sacred and the secular. All of their life is dedicated to serving Allah/God. This is why the suicide bombers are so willing to die and so effective at killing. Their faith has taught them that when they die, they go straight to heaven and eternal life.

In America, we have a slightly different take on life and death issues. We have determined that the war is for our national good and is separate from our spiritual well-being. This is why our president can call it a "just" war. He is only trying to protect our "national" system of government. But the death of every soldier and civilian in this war is of great matter to God! And it is causing pain and grief and lifelong adjustments to every affected family on both sides of the war.

Now, when we bring this same mindset to the church, we can see why my little sister, her sister, myself, and so many other women are sacrificed for the good of "the system." People have lined up to stay with the "power" section of the system. Many people are confused that all "pastors/priests" are holy men of God and that "the system" must protect them, for God's sake. Yes! Of course it is a confused thought process. Systems, however, are self-perpetuating! Every system is subject to dysfunction. And domestic violence, a system dysfunction, is a sin before God!

> Church leaders and seminary administrators could have taken steps to prevent (pastors) from abusing again. Those in power could have required rigorous supervision and could have insisted on accountability and restitution. They could have provided support for me through counseling and by upholding their own policies. In that way an environment of safety would have been created for others seeking healing from abuse. Such actions would have been steps toward redeeming an unjust situation. Instead, their decision not to act but to protect their own and to hush up the incidents superseded any notion of redemption. Thus, more injustice was inflicted, a great deal more.[1]

In Christianity, the individual comes before the system! In Christianity and in a true democracy, Christ died to guarantee the value, worth, and the significance of *every individual.* This is the gift of salvation.

Salvation requires confession, repentance, acceptance, the infilling of the Holy Spirit, authentic worship, daily devotion, and true praise. Salvation demands that we become part of the healing ministry that Jesus launched in the world. Salvation requires that every local congregation become a healing station where love, care, nurture, and wholeness are the benchmarks. Salvation demands that the sin of domestic violence stop in God's house of prayer for all people! Salvation pulls the local church beyond being a simple clog in an ineffective, nonpersonal system! The local church only serves as a "filling station" for the individuals who attend. God *does* need our help in keeping the systems all working together, functioning properly, and in harmony. God *does not* need our help in protecting those who are taking advantage of their offices. God *does not* need our help in perpetuating the work of Jesus Christ via stained and unholy means. God *does* need our help in having open eyes, open compassionate hearts, listening spirits, and speaking mouths to come to the aid of every victim within God's family.

One of my favorite stories about a sick family system is that of Much Afraid Fearing, a little, crippled lamb who wanted to go to work for the Good Shepherd. She was born into the Fearing family. How in the world could a little, crippled sheep, named Much Afraid Fearing, go to the High Places and be of service to anyone? But, she was a determined little crippled sheep.[2]

Much Afraid's family got wind of her decision to escape their grasp and decided that the very best thing that they could do for this little crippled and confused sheep was to find her a good spouse. So they went to work and made arrangements to marry Much Afraid to her distant cousin, Mr. Craven-Fear. If she married this sheep, she realized that her name would be Much Afraid Craven-Fear. So the little, crippled sheep decided to make a run for the mountains. She refused to remain within her sick family system.

From somewhere this act of courage broke through her reality. From some place, way down deep on the inside, the little crippled sheep knew that her life was not to be lived in the valley with a group of relatives who were all controlled by their anxieties and fears. Something within Much Afraid, told her to go! Something within this little crippled sheep rose to her conscious mind and decided that there was more for her away from her family. So, as they locked her in her bedroom, and sat outside to keep her in line, she broke out of the bedroom window and began the long trek to the high places. Would you believe that the Good Shepherd met her along the way?

"Much Afraid," the Good Shepherd asked, "where are you headed?" Much Afraid, replied, "I must go to the high places, where I can work with you." "Well," said the Good Shepherd, "If you are determined to go, I'm going to give you some company to help you make the journey." Suddenly, there stood two tall women, dressed in all black, with wide hats and veils covering their faces. One woman's name was Suffering. The other woman's name was Sorrow. The Good Shepherd said to Much Afraid, "These two women do not talk. But they will ensure that you will reach the high places, since you are determined, go!"

Hannah Hurnard wrote this allegory about the life of every Christian who has been commanded to "Go into all the world and make disciples" (Matt. 28:19). *Hinds' Feet on High Places* ought to be mandatory reading for every new convert to local congregations. And, it ought to be on the recommended reading list for every woman's ministry in local congregations. For it outlines for us the process that is too often required as we move about within our local congregational walls as well as when we return into the world where we live, work, play, and touch the lives of others.

Hannah's tale says that all of us are like the first disciples, afraid. Hannah's story tells us that each one of us is actually named Much Afraid. If we seriously look at that crippled little sheep's willingness to break out of her comfort zone, we will be forced to both repent and to confess as we prepare to break out of ours! For the majority of us are way too comfortable attending worship on Sunday morning and staying locked within our little "let's make pretend that all is right with the world" boxes for the rest of the week. This is one of the logical moves within each and every system, including the church.

But this is a brand new season in the church. This is the season of change. This is the season of awareness. And, this is the season of the women in the church being awakened and revived. So the Word of God comes to say to every Much Afraid within the church, "It's time to bust out, make a move, and go on to wholeness!"

Matthew 28 is the passage of scripture where the farewell benediction of Jesus is given to the small group of "sheep" to whom he had been rabbi, teacher, miracle worker, friend, and now the resurrected Savior. These are the words that Jesus said as he got ready to return to God and prepare to send the power of the Holy Spirit to walk with them to the high places. These are the words of institution for the church of Jesus Christ. These are the words that will usher in a different type of system within the world.

Jesus sums up this new ministry with a few words. Jesus blesses and then commissions the disciples with a few words. Jesus lets them know that the church is now left in their hand with a few words. These few words are the last will, testament, and legacy of Jesus Christ. They are found in the very last chapter of Matthew's Gospel as the evangelist wraps up his story of the Jewish carpenter on the day of his ascension and return to God.

Eugene Peterson's *The Message* reads like this:

> Meanwhile the eleven disciples were on their way to Galilee, headed for the mountain Jesus had set for their reunion. The moment they saw Jesus they worshiped him. Some though, held back, not sure about worship about risking themselves totally.
>
> Jesus, undeterred, went right ahead and gave his charge: "God authorized and commanded me to commission you: Go out and train everyone you meet, far and near, in this way of life, marking them for baptism in the threefold name: Creator, Son, and Holy Spirit. Then instruct them in the practice of all I have commanded you. I'll be with you as you do this, day after day after day, right up to the end of the age (Matt. 28:16–20)."

Like the disciples, we worship Jesus with our mouths while there is great fear in our hearts. The first church and the current church of Jesus Christ is filled with skeptical, doubtful, Much Afraid sheep. We are a group of people who know about Jesus. We have a nodding acquaintance with God. But, for the most part, we are afraid to trust the Risen Savior. It is obvious that we are afraid, for the average local body of believers is weak and anemic and has very little power to effect change in the world. Most of us are afraid to challenge the sick system that we see at work.

Yet, we *have a story to tell to the nations!* We have a commandment from the one who role-modeled for us what resurrection, getting up from a place of death, and moving on is all about. This Jesus—who walked the dusty shores of earthly villages, fed thousands, healed so many, performed miracles, invited others into his power circle, and then willingly died at the hands of a turncoat mob—rose again to show us that every plot to dominate, suppress, manipulate, control, oppress, and even kill us will not win!

We have the personal story about this Jesus who came into our hearts one day, by faith, turned our lives around, took us from the gutter of life, breathed upon us the re-creating power of transformation, changed our habits, changed our associations, changed our desires, and changed our lives. We have been called into a system of abundant life! Yet we are Much Afraid, and not willing to go. Too often we have been afraid of rocking the system. Too often we have sat silent and seen other women hurt by the internal system that is in place to quiet any ruckus. Too often we have been part of the pain that other women have experienced in the church of the Living God!

My sisters, we have a problem. We have a problem in that this passage is not an invitation for our debate and consideration. We have a problem in that when we fail to follow the commands of the Good Shepherd, and to walk with Suffering and Sorrow to the high places, we too are in violation of our covenantal obligations and that is S-I-N! God's church does not grow when we don't get up and move from dead places where abuse is active and misuse of women and children is tolerated; when we don't call our local bodies to responsibility for seeing us, hearing us, and responding to our pain. And, if the local body is not growing, then it is dying and decaying and the stench of death is setting in, little by little.

Jesus Christ has called you and me to be part of a healing system. In these few verses, we have all that we need supplied. First, we can trust our Savior! We all have some past records of how Jesus Christ has worked issues and situations out for us in days gone by. We all have some ancestors who testified that Jesus Christ has made ways out of no ways and opened doors that they could not see. We too serve this risen Savior. This same Jesus remains trustworthy. We do not trust any system! Our faith is in Jesus Christ, who came to break down systems, strongholds, and walls.

Second, we have a source of power whose name is the Holy Spirit. Acts 1:8 says, "You will receive power when the Holy Spirit has come upon you." The Holy Spirit is the third person of the Trinity. The Holy Spirit's function is to remind us of what Jesus has taught. Jesus taught that each individual is worthwhile, precious, and worth his death on the cross! Jesus taught that we don't have to die. He came so that we might live.

The Holy Spirit comes to validate the Word of God. The Holy Spirit comes to impart to us the ability to say "No" to the dominion of sin in our lives and on our lives. The Holy Spirit comes to separate us from the old ways, the victim stance, and to set us apart for the abundant living of these days. The Holy Spirit comes to inspire us, to breathe upon us, to breath through the church, and to breath among us as we gather. The Holy Spirit comes to transform us by the renewing of our minds. The Holy Spirit comes to activate our wills to follow the command to go into the world spreading the news of a new and different way to live. The Holy Spirit reminds us of our obligation to get out of our comfort zones and move out into the big and scary world. The Holy Spirit comes to bring us new revelations of how free we can really become. The Holy Spirit comes to help us to see what we could not see before and to open our eyes and allow us to see what we were blinded to before. And the Holy Spirit comes to touch our hands so that we will want to become part of the healing ministry of Christ in the world that affects us and that we affect.

Each one of us has about 250 people that we will come in contact with and have within our sphere of influence. Sales companies know that there are people they can get to listen to their sales pitch and assist them in making a sale. This is why sales people often ask clients to provide names of friends so that they can have other leads. These are the very same people whom Jesus expects that you will talk to, get to listen to you, assist them in going in life-affirming directions. Then you are to influence them by your life into becoming new, better, and more committed disciples.

The entire substance of our task as Christians is to be followers of Christ; to share God's goodness with others; to allow the life that we live to be a witness to others; and to bring others to Christ. This means that I have a personal relationship with Jesus Christ and that my talk is consistent with my walk. When I was doing my internship at Gorham United Methodist Church in Chicago, I shared an office with an older associate pastor whose name is Rev. Mildred Crutchfield. She began to ask questions about my missing spouse. In those days, Mista Chuck was a member of the "CME Church." He came to Gorham on Christmas, Mother's Day, and Easter to watch the children perform! Mista Chuck was an alcoholic in those days and I was living in a situation that was not life-affirming. Mista Chuck was not a physically violent man, but he was both mentally and verbally abusive. Mildred knew that I was not filled with abundant life. She never asked me about my home life. She just opened her eyes and saw!

Rev. Mildred Crutchfield, an older widow, had heard the command to "Go." Every Saturday, she began to call Mista Chuck to invite him to attend worship at Gorham. On many occasions, Mista Chuck did not want to talk to Rev. Mildred. On many occasions, he got angry when I would hand him the phone and say, "It's Rev. Crutchfield." But Rev. Mildred had heard the call to "go and to make disciples."

Finally, Mista Chuck decided to heed Rev. Crutchfield's invitation. I can't take credit for the day that Mista Chuck walked down the aisle and joined the church. It was Rev. Mildred who had taken seriously the call to "Go," even if it meant going via the telephone. It was not a "magic" moment. It was not an instant process. But God worked in the life of Mista Chuck. The Holy Spirit put a rod of steel within my back. As he said, "No" to alcohol, I had to learn to say "No" to mental and verbal abuse! I know Suffering and Sorrow! We walked to the high place. Today, I would not trade this awesome spouse of mine. But it was not always so.

Jesus gave us a healing strategy. We are to be baptized into the death of the old ways and to teach new disciples how to fully live for Christ. This means that we have to both identify them with

Jesus Christ through water baptism and then with follow-up classes in discipleship. Just taking a trip to an altar does not a Christian make. That is a convert. It is in the days following that important step that the disciple is formed as we teach by our words and, more importantly, by our lives.

Finally, Jesus gave us the support of his promise and his presence as we journey to the High Places. Much Afraid, we don't go alone. "I'll be with you always even to the end of the age." We can refuse to stay in situations where domestic violence is the norm. We can stop being the willing victim. We can stand up, walk away, and even begin all over again. We can speak out. We can demand to be visible. We can require accountability of those who have abused us and those who continue to perpetuate the system of oppression. We can go in the midst of our doubts and fears. We can go in the face of a failing economy and war raging all over the world, even within our personal world. We can go without all the answers and with few of the solutions. Our job is to go and to tell our story. The real job of opening eyes and ears and providing resources is left up to the capable Holy Spirit.

Much Afraid wanted to go, and so she was assigned two companions with a promise. Suffering and Sorrow will walk with you to the High Places. Ours is not an easy task, for these companions are with each and every one of us. We have to realize and to appreciate that Suffering and Sorrow help us to climb higher and higher toward the abode of the Good Shepherd. I will not tell you all the story of Hind's Feet, but I will tell you that these two companions' names were changed at the end of the story as well as Much Afraid's. I told Jesus that it would be alright if he changed my name too!

This is the season of system change in the church. And this is the season of revival, renewal, and repentance. For Much Afraid cannot sit and wait to be overcome by Craven-Fear. Much Afraid must bust a move, climb out of the comfortable box, and take off knowing that God has already provided all that she will need along the journey. Our job is to make disciples. We do it one woman at a time. We do it one child at a time. We do it one person at a time. We do it one relative, one neighbor, and one friend at a time. We don't do it because we have been nominated to the evangelism committee! We do it because God has been our help and allowed us to wake up and to make a conscious decision to dismiss all types of abuse and any sort of violence from our lives. How can we but help to tell others about the goodness of our God?

We have a Savior. We have a source of power. We have the substance of the task of every Much Afraid Christian. We have a strategy that is already in place. We have the best support team in the world. God is for us. Jesus died for us to live. And there are legions of angels cheering us to take the trip to the High Place.

On your mark! Get set! It is time for you and me to "Go!" to work helping wipe out domestic violence in all forms. We can do it, for the command has already gone forth. So make up your mind and follow me by asking the abused sister that you know to worship with you next week. The very next friend who calls me whining, not living the abundant life, I am going to invite her to worship with me next week. The very next person who stops to talk with me in the grocery line, at the pharmacy counter, or in the doctor's office, I am inviting that person to worship with me next week. For I am becoming a one woman liberation army and the local body where I attend is becoming more and more a station of healing for all people, especially for women and their children!

There is a place of victimization within each one of us. Currently within each one of us there is something that is difficult for us to recall, remember, and deal with. Within each one of us, from our past, is a hurt place that just will not seem to heal. Within each one of us there is an emptiness that food, sex, drugs, and abusive situations cannot fill. Well, Jesus is the answer for the world today. Above him there is no other, for Jesus is the Way, the Truth, and the Life! In the name of Jesus, our Resurrected Savior, I just strongly urge all of us to simply get up and go to work. We must eradicate domestic violence and all of its friends—mental abuse, emotional damage, spiritual sacrilege, and physical harm—from within God's houses across the world. All that we need, God's hand has already provided. All heavenly systems are go! Great is God's faithfulness unto every Much Afraid. And that is mighty good news!

REFLECTIONS

- Could you believe the letter that started this chapter? When have you heard a story like this one before?

- Do you have any personal experience being the victim of a "system"?

- What are your thoughts about personally impacting "systems" to recognize the significance of women and children?

- What was the most important thing that you have learned from this book?

- How will you change your life to become a more effective advocate for the elimination of domestic violence?

Epilogue

SISTER,
SAVE YOURSELF

Dear One,

We have come to the end of another venture in sharing through the written pages. Please know that you have been and continue to be in my daily prayers. You are so important to me. It is because of you that I spend long hours in research, study, and meditation, so that we can become more equipped to be the agents of change that we want to see in our world. It is essential that you and I make a permanent, positive impact upon our world.

Vital awareness about the sin of domestic violence is not the end of our shared journey. Now the time has come that we must put feet and action to our new consciousness. It is my prayer that you will covenant with God to share something that you have learned with another sister or brother. Find an agency, a shelter, an established community ministry that is assisting women who are committed to being free from the pain of domestic violence. Join them to learn more and to be a partner in this necessary fight.

My intention has been to show my readers that God is on our side and our escape from victimization is already a done deal. By the stripes of Jesus we are already healed. Abundant life is ours for the accepting. By the resurrection of Jesus Christ the power to get up, walk on, and live in victory is ours. Yet we have to make the first step to recognize that a new reality can be ours, by faith and by our works.

You and I are never alone. Surely, goodness and mercy do follow us all the days of our lives. And we shall dwell in the healing house of God throughout eternity—an eternity that is already in progress!

CLOSING PRAYER

Transcendent and Immanent Sovereign,

Thank you for another opportunity to explore your Living Word, your intentions for our life, and the multiple paths you have opened for our exploration to wholeness. We approach you with gratitude for the living of our days, for the folks who have taught us so many lessons, and for the church, which has been both blessing and curse throughout our lives.

The pain of women and children causes our hearts great sorrow, God. The many and diverse methods of oppression, depression, suppression, and violence against us is a source of unceasing anguish. For we recognize that whenever people are denied their basic human rights it is sin! We are people of your holy and divine covenant. We can now better affirm that you are on our side. You never leave us alone.

God of glory and power, we come to you for assistance and clarity about how we can help ourselves and our sisters around the world to become free to experience abundant life. Too often the pain of our hearts, minds, and spirits has caused us to rely upon our own resources, causing us to stray further away from you and your compassionate love. Forgive us of our sin. Restore us to right relationship with you and with our sisters. Shine in us so that others might truly see how our adoption into your royal family brings life, liberty, and joy in the Holy Spirit.

We thank you for the gift of Jesus Christ, who is our blessing, our comfort, and our healer. We have finished this book to continue our journey to holy living. We leave this time of name changing, from victim to survivor, assured that you go before us and live in us. We leave this book, challenged to give unto others what we have received. Help us to be open to every opportunity to glorify your name in grace, power, and security, as we pray in the matchless name of Jesus Christ. And it is so!

Until we meet the next time,
Shalom!
Sista Linda
Woman to Woman Ministries, Inc.
Saving sisters, one woman at a time! Join us!

Appendix

A SERVICE OF HEALING MEMORIES

LEADER 1: Glory to God the Creator, who makes the story.
Glory to the Son, who tells the story.
Glory to the Spirit, who inspires the story.
Glory to God, the Three in One, who has gathered us to share our common story.
My prayer is that we may experience God's compassion, love, and healing power in this hour of worship. Welcome.

LEADER 2: My prayer is that God will so bless our worship that it will fill our hearts with gladness and holiness as we recall every victim of domestic violence—those who died from domestic violence; those who continue to live with the fear and the pain of domestic violence, especially with local congregations; our loved ones; and each other. Let us receive from this worship increased strength and guidance for the living of our days. We thank you for allowing us to pray with you. It is our hope that the spirit of this Service of Healing Memories will spread blessings galore over all of our days. Welcome to the gathered presence of God's people. Let's prepare our hearts for worship.

CALL TO WORSHIP

LEADER 1: In the beginning, God created Eve and called her "the mother of all."

PEOPLE: We remember Eve. We remember the finger of blame pointed at her, the pain it caused, and the abuse she has carried for generations. We also remember God's promise that through her salvation would come to the earth. Heal every Eve of her pain.

LEADER 2: The story of the matriarchs includes the tale of Leah. Her father mistreated her; her husband hated her; and the strife between she and her sister was never settled.

PEOPLE: We remember Leah. We remember how she has left a legacy of women having babies, trying to win the hearts of men. We also remember that God saw her plight and made her the mother of the tribe of Judah, whose praise we uplift. Heal every Leah of her pain.

LEADER 1: The history of the church includes Hannah, a woman abused by church and society, because of her inability to bear a child.

PEOPLE: We remember Hannah. The first biblical prayer of a woman is hers, as she petitioned God for a son. She promised to give her child back to God; and Samuel, her son, was the first prophet and priest. We also remember the pain of all women who long for children. Heal every Hannah of her pain.

LEADER 2: Rizbah is a name seldom called. She is the foremother of Harriet Tubman, Sojourner Truth, and Rosa Parks. Her standing for the entire community is legend.

PEOPLE: We remember Rizbah. We remember how she stood alone for five months, guarding not only the bodies of her two sons, but, the five sons of others. She stood until God sent rain to refresh the land. The reign of justice in our world is due, in great measure, to women like her who are bold enough to challenge injustice and stand alone. Heal every Rizbah from her pain.

LEADER 1: We praise military leaders and applaud their mighty exploits. When we do the name of Deborah must be lifted.

PEOPLE: We remember Deborah. We remember her hesitation in leaving her traditional and accepted roles of wife and mother to lead Israel into a winning battle. Onto the battlefield she went, her example encouraging other women to follow God into uncharted areas. Heal every Deborah of her pain.

LEADER 2: We remember the abused, neglected, and unnamed women, whose stories are important, though not often told.

PEOPLE: We remember women. We remember those filled with fears and anxieties. We remember the hurt, the rejected, and the depressed. We remember those with broken dreams, crushed spirits, and aching hearts. Today we pause to remember all women. Heal every woman of her pain.

LEADER 1: We remember the significant women in our lives.

PEOPLE: We remember our nurturers. We remember mothers, sisters, grandmothers, sister-mothers, community-mothers, church-mothers, teacher-mothers, and friend-mothers. We remember their sacrifices of love, hugs, food, care, and role-modeling. We remember that they had painful experiences, unrealistic expectations, and wounds of their own. They had high hopes, dreams, and visions of a day when their hearts could soar. Today, for who they were and are, we remember, with love and thanksgiving, the significant contributions of women! God bless women! God heal women. God stop the domestic violence against women with our help, our prayers, and our refusal to any longer participate as victims!

CALL TO CONFESSION

LEADER 2: There is a crisis in our community. Domestic violence is alive and well. This is not a new realization, for women and their children are suffering every day. Many of them have died. We know that there can be no sunshine theology for people who live in stormy weather! We are here as advocates against any further violence. Let us ask forgiveness for our sin of silence in the past.

SILENT PRAYER

COMMON CONFESSION

LEADER 1: We gather this day as living signs of your great grace, Almighty God. For it could have been us in many of the abusive situations where violence reared its ugly head. We can remember too well the times when we experienced violence and said nothing and when we saw violence and remained silent. God, forgive us our sin. Grant unto us voice and power. Give us deeds of compassion to express. Help us to do the acts of love that you desire. We ask these blessings in the name of Jesus, the Healer.

A DANCE OF LIFE!

Liturgical dancers

A SPEECH OF ADVOCACY OR A HOMILY

A SONG OF LIFE!

Special guest soloist

OFFERTORY INVITATION

LEADER 1: God, who is Life-giver and Nurturer, is our provider, El Shaddai, the multibreasted one. From the more than enough, which we have already received, let's share in love the names of every domestic abuse survivor who died in the midst of struggling to be free. And let us offer the name of every woman who continues the journey, wanting to be free from violence of all sorts. God, hear our prayers.

OFFERTORY PRAISE

LEADER 2: Womb of being, in you we live, move, and have our being. We have been sustained through you. Let our gifts of memory, hope, and finances be used to nourish others, we pray in the name that cannot be limited, the name of Jesus Christ. Amen.

CALL TO OFFER INTENTIONS FOR HURTING WOMEN

LEADER 1: The prophet Jeremiah called for the wise and cunning women to come and lament for us. Today we will call out names and offer intentional prayers on behalf of our sisters.

PEOPLE: **Thank God for women who have cried and prayed for us.**

LEADER: The Wisdom of God called a righteous women more valuable than precious jewels.

PEOPLE: **Thank God for women who have modeled hope and wholeness for us.**

LEADER: Jesus said, "Wherever the good news is shared, it will be told in memory of her," a woman who ministered unto him. Let us take this time to call out those names of women who are upon our hearts. (A time of name calling follows.)

LEADER: The Ancient of Days is open to receive our prayers.

PEOPLE: **Thank God for all of the women whose service in God's name has been a blessing to us! God, hear our prayers. Amen.**

A CLOSING SONG OF COMMUNITY

(Consider using Sweet Honey in the Rock's "Run," on their twenty-fifth anniversary CD entitled . . . *twenty-five*.)

BENEDICTION

LEADER 2: We are signs of life to those who seek hope.

PEOPLE: **We will lift our voices, dance our dance, and sing our song of life.**

LEADER: We are the women who will not be quiet.

PEOPLE: **We will lift our voices, dance our dance, and sing our song of life.**

LEADER: Go into the world; be encouraged that all the lovely things you do are signs of God, alive and continually at work, in the world.

PEOPLE: **We leave to be signs of life, advocating, dancing, and singing our way to a new reality where domestic violence is no more!**

ALL: The new future is already here. It is so!

(One of the leaders invites the people to be seated for a time of silent reflection as the musician plays a soft postlude, then dismisses them to a time of refreshments and sharing.)

NOTES

Acknowledgements

1. Marie Fortune, *Sexual Violence: The Sin Revisited* (Cleveland: Pilgrim Press, 2005), 70–71.

2. Phenessa A. Gray, "I'm Through Crying," *My Soul's Surrender* (Bloomington, Ind.: AuthorHouse, 2002), 3. Used by permission of the author.

Chapter 1

1. Alice Walker, "They were women then," from *All the Women Are White, All the Blacks Are Men, But Some of Us Are Brave: Black Women's Studies*, ed. Gloria T. Hull, Patricia Bell Scott, and Barbara Smith (Old Westbury, N.Y.: Feminist Press, 1982).

2. Nannie Helen Burrough's pamplet, "Who Started Women's Day," in Cheryl Townsend Gilkes, *If It Wasn't for the Women* (Maryknoll, N.Y.: Orbis Books, 2001), 114.

3. Gilkes, *If It Wasn't for the Women,* 210.

4. Teresa L. Fry Brown, *God Don't Like Ugly* (Nashville: Abingdon Press, 2000), 90–91.

5. Brown, *God Don't Like Ugly,* 42.

6. Delores Williams, *Sisters in the Wilderness: The Challenge of Womanist God-Talk,* (Maryknoll, N.Y.: Orbis Books, 1993).

7. Dr. Dorothy I. Height, *Open Wide the Freedom Gates* (New York: PublicAffairs, 2003).

Chapter 4

1. Oswald Chambers, *My Utmost for His Highest* (Grand Rapids, Mich.: Discovery House, 1992), June 28.

2. Ibid.

Chapter 6

1. Marie Fortune, *Keeping the Faith* (San Francisco: HarperSanFrancisco, 1987), 18–19.

Chapter 8

1. Kelly Brown Douglas, *Sexuality and the Black Church* (New York: Orbis Books, 1999), 116.

Chapter 9

1. Kelly Brown Douglas, *Sexuality and the Black Church* (New York: Orbis Books, 1999), 123.

Chapter 10

1. Nancy Werking Poling, *Victim to Survivor: Women Recovering from Clergy Sexual Abuse* (Cleveland: United Church Press, 1999), 19–20.

2. Hannah Hurnard, *Hinds' Feet on High Places* (Wheaton, Ill.: Living Books, 1986).

Other books from The Pilgrim Press

LIVING BOUNTIFULLY
The Blessings of Responsible Stewardship
LINDA H. HOLLIES
0-8298-1676-3/paper/128 pages/$16.00

Jesus spent a great deal of time speaking to his followers about money and property. Hollies feels that—like Jesus—this is an issue that women in general and women of color in particular need to talk about and address in their personal lives. In *Living Bountifully,* Hollies shares her lessons, strategies, and experiences of godly stewardship.

ON THEIR WAY TO WONDERFUL
A Journey with Ruth and Naomi
LINDA H. HOLLIES
0-8298-1604-6/paper/130 pages/$18.00

This resource is an exploration of multicultural marriage (Ruth and Boaz) as well as diversity and racism in Scripture (Ruth, a Moabite whom God allows to enter the forbidden Jewish bloodline). Women will relate to this book as it touches on issues that impact their lives, such as making critical decisions, handling relationships, and renewal of self and soul.

BODACIOUS WOMANIST WISDOM
LINDA H. HOLLIES
0-8298-1529-5/paper/144 pages/$18.00

Hollies takes a look at the "bodaciousness" of women of color through biblical stories of specific women such as the "bent over woman" in Luke 13, Queen Esther, Mary, and several unnamed biblical women. Each chapter ends with a "Woman Wisdom Speaks" quote from Scripture and "Womanist Wisdom" and "Bodacious Woman" words.

To order these or any other books from The Pilgrim Press call or write to:

THE PILGRIM PRESS
700 PROSPECT AVENUE EAST
CLEVELAND, OHIO 44115-1100

Phone orders: 1-800-537-3394 ▪ Fax orders: 216-736-2206
Please include shipping charges of $5.00 for the first book and $0.75 for each additional book.
Or order from our web sites at www.thepilgrimpress.com and www.ucpress.com.

Prices subject to change without notice.